Google Sh[...] Custom Functions with Apps Script

Over 150 Apps Script Code Examples for Sheets

By

Laurence Lars Svekis

Dedicated to

Alexis and Sebastian

Thank you for your support

For more content and to learn more, visit

https://basescripts.com/

Book Source Code on GitHub
https://github.com/lsvekis/Sheets-Custom-Formulas-Book

1 : Mastering Basic Custom Functions

In this opening chapter, we introduce the foundational concepts of Google Apps Script for custom functions in Google Sheets. Begin by learning how to create simple functions that perform calculations such as summing ranges, generating unique codes, and converting data types. Each section includes sample data, a step-by-step guide to implementing the function, and practical exercises to enhance your learning.

Function for Summing Up Specific Ranges

A12		fx =SUM_OVER_THRESHOLD(A1:A11, 50)		
	A	B	C	D
1	**A**	**B**	**C**	**D**
2	10			
3	55			
4	65			
5	30			
6	75			
7	20			
8	40			
9	85			
10	25			
11	95			
12	375			

Sample Data: SUM_OVER_THRESHOLD

A	B
10	
55	
65	

30	
75	
20	
40	
85	
25	
95	

Objective: Write a custom function that sums the values in a specified range, but only if they are greater than a certain value.

Learning Outcomes:
- Understand the syntax for defining custom functions.
- Learn to manipulate cell ranges and arrays.
- Apply conditional logic to filter out unwanted data.

Code Example:

```
/**
 * Returns the sum of numbers in a given range that are
greater than a specified threshold.
 *
 * @param {range} data The range to sum over.
 * @param {number} threshold The minimum value to include
in the sum.
 * @return {number} The sum of the numbers greater than the
threshold.
 * @customfunction
 */
function SUM_OVER_THRESHOLD(data, threshold) {
  return data.flat().filter(val => typeof val === 'number' &&
val > threshold).reduce((sum, val) => sum + val, 0);
}
```

Steps:
1. Open a Google Sheet and go to Extensions > Apps Script to open the Apps Script editor.

2. Create a new project or use an existing one, and paste the code above into the script.
3. Save your changes and return to the Sheet.
4. Input some numerical data in a range, e.g., A1:A10.
5. In an empty cell, test the function with the formula: =SUM_OVER_THRESHOLD(A1:A10, 50). Replace 50 with your desired threshold.

Expected Result: The function will return the sum of all numbers in the range that are greater than the threshold.

Function to Concatenate and Format Strings

A1:B5	▾	fx Alice	
	A	**B**	**C**
1	Alice	Smith	Alice, Smith
2	Bob	Johnson	Bob, Johnson
3	Charlie	Brown	Charlie, Brown
4	Dave	Wilson	Dave, Wilson
5	Eve	Taylor	Eve, Taylor

Sample Data: CONCATENATE_WITH_SEPARATOR

Alice	Smith
Bob	Johnson
Charlie	Brown
Dave	Wilson
Eve	Taylor

Objective: Write a function that concatenates strings from two different columns and formats the output.

Learning Outcomes:
- Learn how to manipulate strings.
- Understand the concept of joining and formatting data.

Code Example:

```
/**
 * Concatenates values from two columns with a separator.
 *
 * @param {range} col1 The first column of strings.
 * @param {range} col2 The second column of strings.
 * @param {string} separator The separator string.
 * @return {array} The concatenated and formatted strings.
 * @customfunction
 */
function CONCATENATE_WITH_SEPARATOR(col1, col2,
separator) {
const result = [];
for (let i = 0; i < Math.min(col1.length, col2.length); i++) {
result.push([col1[i][0] + separator + col2[i][0]]);
}
return result;
}
```

Steps:
1. Open the Apps Script editor from the Google Sheet.
2. Create a new project or use an existing one, and paste the code above into the script.
3. Save the changes and go back to the Sheet.
4. Enter text data in two columns, e.g., A1:A5 and B1:B5.
5. Use the function with a formula like =CONCATENATE_WITH_SEPARATOR(A1:A5, B1:B5, ", ").

Expected Result: The output will be a new column where the values from both columns are combined and separated by the provided separator.

Function to Calculate Days Until a Future Date

B1	▼	_fx_ =DAYS_TO_FUTURE_DATE(A1)	

	A	B	C
1	2024-06-01	10	
2	2024-07-15	54	
3	2024-12-25	217	
4	2025-01-01	224	
5	2025-04-01	314	

Sample Data: DAYS_TO_FUTURE_DATE

2024-06-01
2024-07-15
2024-12-25
2025-01-01
2025-04-01

Objective: Write a function that calculates the number of days from today to a given date.

Learning Outcomes:

- Learn to work with date objects and calculate time intervals.
- Understand how to handle and validate input data.

Code Example:

```
/**
 * Calculates the number of days from today to a specified
future date.
 *
 * @param {date} futureDate The future date to compare
against today.
 * @return {number} The number of days from today to the
specified future date.
 * @customfunction
 */
function DAYS_TO_FUTURE_DATE(futureDate) {
 const today = new Date();
```

```
const date = new Date(futureDate);
const diffTime = date - today;
const diffDays = Math.ceil(diffTime / (1000 * 60 * 60 * 24));
return diffDays >= 0 ? diffDays : "Date is in the past!";
}
```

Steps:
1. Open the Apps Script editor from the Google Sheet.
2. Create a new project or use an existing one, and paste the code above into the script.
3. Save the changes and return to the Sheet.
4. Provide a future date in a cell, e.g., A1 with a value like 2024-06-01.
5. Use the custom function:
   =DAYS_TO_FUTURE_DATE(A1).

Expected Result: The function will return the number of days between today and the specified future date or a warning message if the date is in the past.

Calculate and Categorize Average

A11	▾	fx =AVERAGE_WITH_CATEGORY(A1:A8, 30, 70)					
	A	B	C	D	E	F ▾	G
1	10						
2	20						
3	35						
4	45						
5	55						
6	65						
7	75						
8	85						
9	95						
10	105						
11	Average 48.75, Category: Medium						

Sample Data: AVERAGE_WITH_CATEGORY

10
20
35

14

45
55
65
75
85
95
105

Objective: Write a function to calculate the average of a specified range and categorize it as "Low," "Medium," or "High" based on user-defined thresholds.

Learning Outcomes:
- Learn how to work with statistical functions.
- Understand how to categorize numeric values based on ranges.

Code Example:

```
/**
 * Calculates the average of a range and categorizes it based
on user thresholds.
 *
 * @param {range} data The range of numbers to calculate the
average for.
 * @param {number} lowThreshold The upper limit of the
"Low" category.
 * @param {number} highThreshold The lower limit of the
"High" category.
 * @return {string} The average value and its category.
 * @customfunction
 */
function AVERAGE_WITH_CATEGORY(data,
lowThreshold, highThreshold) {
 const validNumbers = data.flat().filter(val => typeof val ===
'number');
 if (validNumbers.length === 0) return "No numeric data!";
```

```javascript
  const avg = validNumbers.reduce((sum, val) => sum + val,
0) / validNumbers.length;
  let category;
 if (avg < lowThreshold) {
 category = "Low";
 } else if (avg >= highThreshold) {
 category = "High";
 } else {
 category = "Medium";
 }
  return `Average: ${avg.toFixed(2)}, Category: ${category}`;
}
```

Steps:
1. Open the Apps Script editor and add this code to a new project.
2. Save changes and return to Google Sheets.
3. Enter a set of numerical data in a column, e.g., A1:A10.
4. Use the custom function like =AVERAGE_WITH_CATEGORY(A1:A10, 30, 70).

Expected Result: The function will calculate the average of the data and return the category label based on the thresholds provided.

Generate Unique Codes

	A	B	C
1	XZYFDF6L		
2	Q2UUR7PV		
3	R3JV7HU8		
4	TGZKMBVN		
5	3LMYQZ5I		
6	H3J8YAAT		
7	R99JZ04G		
8	I0SPVV6F		
9	7MLQ1T6C		
10	AHOYGC4K		

Sample Data: GENERATE_UNIQUE_CODES

(No input data needed, this function generates its own data.)

Objective: Create a function to generate unique alphanumeric codes for a specified range of rows.

Learning Outcomes:
- Learn to generate random alphanumeric strings.
- Understand the concept of looping through ranges and filling rows.

Code Example:
```
/**
 * Generates unique alphanumeric codes for a specified
number of rows.
 *
 * @param {number} numCodes The number of unique codes
to generate.
 * @param {number} length The length of each code.
 * @return {array} An array of unique alphanumeric codes.
 * @customfunction
 */
function GENERATE_UNIQUE_CODES(numCodes, length) {
```

```
const result = [];
const characters =
'ABCDEFGHIJKLMNOPQRSTUVWXYZ0123456789';
for (let i = 0; i < numCodes; i++) {
let code = '';
for (let j = 0; j < length; j++) {
code += characters.charAt(Math.floor(Math.random() *
characters.length));
}
result.push([code]);
}
return result;
}
```

Steps:
1. Add the provided script to a new Apps Script project.
2. Save the changes and return to Google Sheets.
3. Use the custom function with
=GENERATE_UNIQUE_CODES(10, 8).

Expected Result: This function will generate 10 unique alphanumeric codes of length 8 and display them in adjacent cells.

Extract and Count Words in a Text

A2 ▾ | fx =COUNT_WORDS(A1)

	A	B	C
1	The quick brown fox jumps over the lazy dog		
2	the	2	
3	quick	1	
4	brown	1	
5	fox	1	
6	jumps	1	
7	over	1	
8	lazy	1	
9	dog	1	

COUNT_WORDS

The quick brown fox jumps over the lazy dog

Objective: Write a custom function that extracts distinct words from a string, counts them, and displays the count of each word.

Learning Outcomes:
- Practice string splitting and filtering.
- Learn to count occurrences using an object for mapping.

Code Example:

```
/**
 * Extracts distinct words from a string and counts their occurrences.
 *
 * @param {string} text The text from which to extract words.
 * @return {array} An array of words and their counts.
 * @customfunction
 */
function COUNT_WORDS(text) {
const words = text.toLowerCase().match(/\b\w+\b/g);
if (!words) return "No words found!";

const wordCounts = {};
words.forEach(word => {
wordCounts[word] = (wordCounts[word] || 0) + 1;
});

const result = Object.entries(wordCounts).map(([word,
count]) => [word, count]);
 return result;
}
```

Steps:
1. Add the script above to a new Apps Script project.
2. Save and return to Google Sheets.

3. Input a long text string in a cell, e.g., A1.
4. Use the custom function with =COUNT_WORDS(A1).

Expected Result: The function will return an array where each row contains a word from the text and its count.

Finding the Longest String in a Range

A2			fx =LONGEST_STRING(A1:D1)		
	A	B	C	D
1	Short	Moderate	Longer	Longest
2	Moderate			

Sample Data: LONGEST_STRING

Short	Moderate	Longer	Longest

Objective: Write a function that finds the longest string in a specified range of cells.

Learning Outcomes:
- Understand how to work with strings in arrays.
- Learn to identify and compare string lengths.

Code Example:

```
/**
* Finds the longest string in a specified range.
*
* @param {range} data The range to search through.
* @return {string} The longest string found in the range.
* @customfunction
*/
function LONGEST_STRING(data) {
let longest = '';
data.flat().forEach(item => {
if (typeof item === 'string' && item.length > longest.length) {
longest = item;
}
});
return longest || "No strings found!";
```

}

Steps:
1. Open the Apps Script editor and add this code to a new project.
2. Save changes and return to Google Sheets.
3. Enter a range of strings, e.g., A1:A10.
4. Use the custom function like =LONGEST_STRING(A1:A10).

Expected Result: This function will return the longest string found in the provided range.

Checking for Duplicate Values

A2	▾	*fx* =FIND_DUPLICATES(A1:J1)	
	A	B	C
1	1	2	3
2	1		
3	2		
4	3		

Sample Data: FIND_DUPLICATES

1	2	3	4	5	1	2	3	6	7

Objective: Create a custom function that checks for duplicate values in a specified range and returns those duplicates.

Learning Outcomes:
- Learn to work with JavaScript objects as hash maps.
- Understand how to efficiently identify duplicates.

Code Example:
```
/**
 * Checks for duplicate values in a specified range.
 *
 * @param {range} data The range of values to check for
duplicates.
 * @return {array} An array of duplicate values found.
 * @customfunction
```

```
*/
function FIND_DUPLICATES(data) {
const flatData = data.flat();
const occurrences = {};
const duplicates = [];

flatData.forEach(item => {
occurrences[item] = (occurrences[item] || 0) + 1;
});

Object.entries(occurrences).forEach(([key, count]) => {
if (count > 1) {
duplicates.push([key]);
}
});

return duplicates.length > 0 ? duplicates : "No duplicates
found!";
}
```

Steps:
1. Add the above code to a new Apps Script project.
2. Save and return to Google Sheets.
3. Input data with some duplicate values in a range, e.g., A1:A10.
4. Use the custom function =FIND_DUPLICATES(A1:A10).

Expected Result: This function will return an array listing all values that appear more than once in the provided range.

Calculate the Fibonacci Sequence

	A	B
A1	▼ *fx* =GENERATE_FIBONACCI(10)	

	A	B
1	0	
2	1	
3	1	
4	2	
5	3	
6	5	
7	8	
8	13	
9	21	
10	34	

Sample Data: GENERATE_FIBONACCI

(No input data needed, this function generates its own data.)

Objective: Write a function to generate a specified number of Fibonacci numbers starting from the first two.

Learning Outcomes:
- Practice working with arrays to generate sequential data.
- Understand the principles of recursion and iterative algorithms.

Code Example:

```
/**
 * Generates a Fibonacci sequence of the given length.
 *
 * @param {number} numTerms The number of terms to
 generate.
 * @return {array} An array of Fibonacci numbers.
 * @customfunction
 */
function GENERATE_FIBONACCI(numTerms) {
  const fib = [0, 1];
```

```
for (let i = 2; i < numTerms; i++) {
  fib.push(fib[i - 1] + fib[i - 2]);
}
return fib.slice(0, numTerms).map(num => [num]);
}
```

Steps:
1. Paste the code into the Apps Script editor and save your changes.
2. Return to Google Sheets.
3. Use the function with =GENERATE_FIBONACCI(10).

Expected Result: The function will return an array containing the first 10 Fibonacci numbers in adjacent cells.

These exercises will help you work more effectively with arrays, hash maps, and sequential data generation in Google Apps Script.

Convert Celsius to Fahrenheit

A2		▼	_fx_ =CELSIUS_TO_FAHRENHEIT(A1:J1)		
	A	B	C	D	
1	-10	0	10	20	
2	14				
3	32				
4	50				
5	68				
6	86				
7	104				
8	122				
9	140				
10	158				
11	176				

Sample Data: CELSIUS_TO_FAHRENHEIT

-10	0	10	20	30	40	50	60	70	80

Objective: Create a custom function that converts temperatures from Celsius to Fahrenheit for a range of data.

Learning Outcomes:
- Practice working with mathematical formulas.

- Understand how to handle numeric input and return processed data.

Code Example:

```
/**
* Converts temperatures from Celsius to Fahrenheit.
*
* @param {range} data The range of temperatures in Celsius
to convert.
* @return {array} An array of temperatures converted to
Fahrenheit.
* @customfunction
*/
function CELSIUS_TO_FAHRENHEIT(data) {
return data.flat().map(celsius => {
if (typeof celsius !== 'number') return "Invalid input";
return [celsius * 9/5 + 32];
});
}
```

Steps:
1. Open the Apps Script editor and paste the code into a new project.
2. Save the changes and return to Google Sheets.
3. Enter a range of temperatures in Celsius, e.g., A1:A10.
4. Use the custom function like =CELSIUS_TO_FAHRENHEIT(A1:A10).

Expected Result: This function will return an array with temperatures converted to Fahrenheit.

Remove Vowels from a String

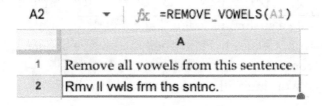

Sample Data: REMOVE_VOWELS

Remove all vowels from this sentence.

Objective: Create a custom function that removes all vowels from a given string.

Learning Outcomes:
- Understand how to manipulate strings using regular expressions.
- Learn to handle edge cases for invalid or empty inputs.

Code Example:

```
/**
 * Removes all vowels from the provided string.
 *
 * @param {string} inputText The input string to process.
 * @return {string} The string with vowels removed.
 * @customfunction
 */
function REMOVE_VOWELS(inputText) {
if (typeof inputText !== 'string') return "Invalid input";
return inputText.replace(/[aeiouAEIOU]/g, '');
}
```

Steps:
1. Paste the code into a new Apps Script project.
2. Save and return to Google Sheets.
3. Enter any string in a cell, e.g., A1.
4. Use the custom function like =REMOVE_VOWELS(A1).

Expected Result: This function will return the string with all vowels removed.

Sum Only Even Numbers

A2   ▾ | *fx* =SUM_EVEN_NUMBERS(A1:J1)

	A	B	C	D	E	F	G	H	I	J
1	1	2	3	4	5	6	7	8	9	10
2	30									

Sample Data: SUM_EVEN_NUMBERS

1	2	3	4	5	6	7	8	9	10

Objective: Create a function that calculates the sum of only even numbers in a given range.

Learning Outcomes:
- Practice using the filter method to process arrays.
- Understand conditional logic to isolate specific values.

Code Example:

```
/**
 * Sums only even numbers from the given range.
 *
 * @param {range} data The range of numbers to sum up.
 * @return {number} The sum of even numbers in the
specified range.
 * @customfunction
 */
function SUM_EVEN_NUMBERS(data) {
 return data.flat().filter(num => typeof num === 'number' &&
num % 2 === 0).reduce((sum, num) => sum + num, 0);
}
```

Steps:
1. Paste the code into a new project in the Apps Script editor.
2. Save the changes and return to Google Sheets.
3. Enter a range of numbers in any column, e.g., A1:A10.
4. Use the function like
   =SUM_EVEN_NUMBERS(A1:A10).

Expected Result: This function will return the sum of only even numbers in the specified range.

Calculate the Median of a Range

| A2 | ▼ | $f\!x$ =MEDIAN_OF_RANGE(A1:J1) |

	A	B	C	D	E	F	G	H	I	J
1	2	4	6	8	10	12	14	16	18	20
2	11									

Sample Data: MEDIAN_OF_RANGE

2	4	6	8	10	12	14	16	18	20

Objective: Create a custom function that calculates the median value from a range of numbers.

Learning Outcomes:
- Understand the concept of sorting and median calculation.
- Learn how to handle cases where the input data is not purely numeric.

Code Example:

```
/**
 * Calculates the median of a given range of numbers.
 *
 * @param {range} data The range of numbers to calculate the
median for.
 * @return {number | string} The median value or an error
message if no valid numbers are found.
 * @customfunction
 */
function MEDIAN_OF_RANGE(data) {
// Filter out non-numeric data and flatten the input array
const numbers = data.flat().filter(val => typeof val ===
'number');

// Check if there are any valid numbers in the range
```

```
if (numbers.length === 0) return "No numeric data!";

// Sort numbers in ascending order
numbers.sort((a, b) => a - b);

// Find the median value
const middle = Math.floor(numbers.length / 2);
return numbers.length % 2 === 0 ? (numbers[middle - 1] +
numbers[middle]) / 2 : numbers[middle];
}
```

Steps:
1. Open the Apps Script editor and paste this code into a new project.
2. Save the script and return to Google Sheets.
3. Enter some numerical data in a range, e.g., A1:A10.
4. Use the function with =MEDIAN_OF_RANGE(A1:A10).

Expected Result: The function will return the median of the specified range or an error message if no valid numbers are found.

Count Uppercase and Lowercase Letters

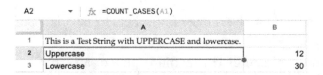

	A	B
1	This is a Test String with UPPERCASE and lowercase.	
2	Uppercase	12
3	Lowercase	30

A2 ƒx =COUNT_CASES(A1)

Sample Data: COUNT_CASES

> This is a Test String with UPPERCASE and lowercase.

Objective: Create a custom function that counts the number of uppercase and lowercase letters in a string.
Learning Outcomes:

- Understand regular expression usage for pattern matching.
- Practice using JavaScript object mappings for counting.

Code Example:

```
/**
 * Counts the number of uppercase and lowercase letters in a
given string.
 *
 * @param {string} inputText The text to count uppercase and
lowercase letters.
 * @return {array} An array with the count of uppercase and
lowercase letters.
 * @customfunction
 */
function COUNT_CASES(inputText) {
if (typeof inputText !== 'string') return "Invalid input";

// Initialize counters for uppercase and lowercase
const upperCount = (inputText.match(/[A-Z]/g) ||
[]).length;
const lowerCount = (inputText.match(/[a-z]/g) || []).length;

return [["Uppercase", upperCount], ["Lowercase",
lowerCount]];
}
```

Steps:
1. Add the code to a new Apps Script project.
2. Save and return to Google Sheets.
3. Enter a text string in a cell, e.g., A1.
4. Use the function with =COUNT_CASES(A1).

Expected Result: The function will return the count of uppercase and lowercase letters in the provided string.

Split Text into Sentences

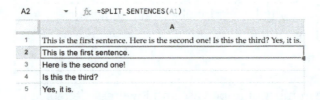

A2	▾	ƒx =SPLIT_SENTENCES(A1)
	A	
1	This is the first sentence. Here is the second one! Is this the third? Yes, it is.	
2	This is the first sentence.	
3	Here is the second one!	
4	Is this the third?	
5	Yes, it is.	

Sample Data: SPLIT_SENTENCES

> This is the first sentence. Here is the second one! Is this the third? Yes, it is.

Objective: Create a custom function that splits a text string into sentences.

Learning Outcomes:
- Learn to work with regular expressions to identify sentence boundaries.
- Practice manipulating strings with arrays.

Code Example:

```
/**
 * Splits the input text into sentences.
 *
 * @param {string} inputText The text to split into sentences.
 * @return {array} An array of sentences extracted from the
input text.
 * @customfunction
 */
function SPLIT_SENTENCES(inputText) {
if (typeof inputText !== 'string') return "Invalid input";

// Regular expression to identify sentences
const sentences = inputText.match(/[^.!?]+[.!?]/g) || [];

// Return sentences as an array of single-item arrays for
Google Sheets
 return sentences.map(sentence => [sentence.trim()]);
}
```

Steps:

1. Paste the code into a new Apps Script project.
2. Save the changes and return to Google Sheets.
3. Enter a long text string in a cell, e.g., A1.
4. Use the function like =SPLIT_SENTENCES(A1).

Expected Result: The function will return an array of sentences extracted from the provided text.

Identify Prime Numbers in a Range

A6   ▾   *fx* =FIND_PRIMES(A1:J5)

	A	B	C	D	E	F	G	H	I	J
1	2	4	6	8	10	12	14	16	18	20
2	3	5	7	11	13	17	19	23	29	31
3	32	33	34	35	36	37	38	39	40	41
4	42	43	44	45	46	47	48	49	50	51
5	52	53	54	55	56	57	58	59	60	61
6	2									
7	3									
8	5									
9	7									
10	11									
11	13									
12	17									

Sample Data: FIND_PRIMES

2	4	6	8	10	12	14	16	18	20
3	5	7	11	13	17	19	23	29	31
32	33	34	35	36	37	38	39	40	41
42	43	44	45	46	47	48	49	50	51
52	53	54	55	56	57	58	59	60	61

Objective: Create a custom function that identifies which numbers in a given range are prime numbers.

Learning Outcomes:

- Practice using conditional logic to identify prime numbers.
- Understand the concept of prime checking through loops.

Code Example:

```
/**
 * Identifies prime numbers in a specified range.
 *
 * @param {range} data The range of numbers to check.
 * @return {array} An array with the prime numbers found.
 * @customfunction
 */
function FIND_PRIMES(data) {
function isPrime(num) {
if (num <= 1) return false;
for (let i = 2; i <= Math.sqrt(num); i++) {
if (num % i === 0) return false;
}
return true;
}

const flatData = data.flat();
const primes = flatData.filter(num => typeof num ===
'number' && isPrime(num));

return primes.length > 0 ? primes.map(prime => [prime]) :
"No primes found!";
}
```

Steps:
1. Paste the code into a new project in the Apps Script editor.
2. Save and return to Google Sheets.
3. Enter a range of numbers, e.g., A1:A10.
4. Use the function with =FIND_PRIMES(A1:A10).

Expected Result: This function will return a list of prime numbers found in the provided range.

2 : Analyzing Data with Advanced Functions

Explore more complex functions that help analyze and interpret data. This chapter covers how to track trends, summarize data, and calculate statistical measures like compound interest and standard deviation. Through practical examples, you will learn to write functions that not only perform calculations but also provide insights into data patterns.

Analyze Yearly Expense Trends

A5	▾	_fx_ =ANALYZE_YEARLY_EXPENSE_TRENDS(A2:A4, B2:D4)		
	A	**B**	**C**	**D**
1	Year	Utilities	Marketing	Research & Development
2	2021	5000	7000	10000
3	2022	5200	6800	9500
4	2023	5400	7200	12000
5	Category 1	Increasing		
6	Category 2	Stable		
7	Category 3	Stable		

Objective: Write a function to analyze the trend in yearly expenses for various categories to determine if they are increasing, decreasing, or remaining stable.

Sample Data:

Year	Utilities	Marketing	Research & Development
2021	5000	7000	10000
2022	5200	6800	9500
2023	5400	7200	12000

Learning Outcomes:
- Learn to compare sequential data to identify trends.

- Practice handling and analyzing data across multiple categories.

Code Example:

```
/**
 * Analyzes yearly expense trends for multiple categories.
 *
 * @param {range} years The range containing years.
 * @param {range} categories The range containing expense
data for each category across multiple years.
 * @return {array | string} An array summarizing the trend for
each category, or an error message if data is invalid.
 * @customfunction
 */
function ANALYZE_YEARLY_EXPENSE_TRENDS(years,
categories) {
const results = [];
const numYears = years.length;
const numCategories = categories[0].length; // Assuming
uniform data
for (let j = 0; j < numCategories; j++) {
let trend = 'Stable';
let increasing = 0;
let decreasing = 0;
for (let i = 1; i < numYears; i++) {
if (categories[i][j] > categories[i - 1][j]) {
increasing++;
} else if (categories[i][j] < categories[i - 1][j]) {
decreasing++;
}
}
if (increasing === numYears - 1) {
trend = 'Increasing';
} else if (decreasing === numYears - 1) {
trend = 'Decreasing';
}
results.push(['Category ' + (j + 1), trend]);
}
```

return results.length > 0 ? results : "No enough data to determine trends.";
}
Steps:
1. Paste the code into a new Apps Script project.
2. Save the changes and return to Google Sheets.
3. Enter the sample data into a format where each column after the first represents a category and each row a year, from A1:D4.
4. Use the function like =ANALYZE_YEARLY_EXPENSE_TRENDS(A2:A4, B2:D4).

Expected Result: The function will provide a trend analysis for each category, indicating whether expenses are increasing, decreasing, or remaining stable over the years.

Track Employee Attendance Streaks

A7	▾	ƒx =TRACK_ATTENDANCE_STREAKS(A2:A6, B2:B6)		
	A	**B**	**C**	**D**
1	Employee	Days Attended Consecutively		
2	Alice	23		
3	Bob	15		
4	Carol	30		
5	David	8		
6	Emily	20		
7	Alice	23 days		
8	Bob	15 days		
9	Carol	30 days		
10	David	8 days		
11	Emily	20 days		

Objective: Develop a function to track the longest streak of daily attendance for each employee over a month.
Sample Data:

Employee	Days Attended Consecutively

Alice	23
Bob	15
Carol	30
David	8
Emily	20

Learning Outcomes:

- Practice calculating streaks or consecutive occurrences.
- Learn to interpret attendance data to assess employee reliability.

Code Example:

```
/**
 * Tracks the longest streak of daily attendance for each
employee.
 *
 * @param {range} employees The range containing employee
names.
 * @param {range} streaks The range containing the number
of consecutive days each employee attended.
 * @return {array | string} An array listing each employee with
their longest attendance streak, or an error message if data is
invalid.
 * @customfunction
 */
function TRACK_ATTENDANCE_STREAKS(employees,
streaks) {
 const results = [];
 for (let i = 0; i < employees.length; i++) {
 const employee = employees[i][0];
 const streak = streaks[i][0];
 results.push([employee, streak + " days"]);
 }
 return results.length > 0 ? results : "Invalid or empty data!";
}
```

Steps:

1. Paste the code into a new Apps Script project.
2. Save the changes and return to Google Sheets.
3. Enter the sample data into columns A1:B6.
4. Use the function like
   =TRACK_ATTENDANCE_STREAKS(A2:A6, B2:B6).

Expected Result: The function will list each employee along with their longest consecutive attendance streak, highlighting their consistency.

Summarize Project Budget Utilization

A7	▾	*fx* =SUMMARIZE_BUDGET_UTILIZATION(A2:A6, B2:B6, C2:C6)		
	A	B	C	D	E
1	Project	Allocated Budget	Spent Amount		
2	Project A	100000	75000		
3	Project B	50000	50000		
4	Project C	75000	55000		
5	Project D	60000	61000		
6	Project E	85000	90000		
7	Project A	75.00%			
8	Project B	100.00%			
9	Project C	73.33%			
10	Project D	101.67%			
11	Project E	105.88%			

Objective: Create a function to summarize how much of the allocated budget has been utilized by each project.

Sample Data:

Project	Allocated Budget	Spent Amount
Project A	100000	75000
Project B	50000	50000
Project C	75000	55000
Project D	60000	61000
Project E	85000	90000

Learning Outcomes:
- Learn to calculate the percentage of budget utilized.

- Practice creating financial summaries to aid in budget management.

Code Example:

```
/**
 * Summarizes budget utilization for each project.
 *
 * @param {range} projects The range containing project
names.
 * @param {range} budgets The range containing allocated
budgets.
 * @param {range} spent The range containing amounts spent.
 * @return {array | string} An array listing each project with its
budget utilization as a percentage, or an error message if data
is invalid.
 * @customfunction
 */
function SUMMARIZE_BUDGET_UTILIZATION(projects,
budgets, spent) {
const results = [];
for (let i = 0; i < projects.length; i++) {
const project = projects[i][0];
const budget = budgets[i][0];
const expenditure = spent[i][0];
const utilization = (expenditure / budget) * 100;
results.push([project, utilization.toFixed(2) + "%"]);
}
return results.length > 0 ? results : "Invalid or empty data!";
}
```

Steps:
1. Paste the code into a new Apps Script project.
2. Save the changes and return to Google Sheets.
3. Enter the sample data into columns A1:C6.
4. Use the function like
   =SUMMARIZE_BUDGET_UTILIZATION(A2:A6,
   B2:B6, C2:C6).

Expected Result: The function will provide a summary of budget utilization for each project, indicating the percentage of the allocated budget that has been spent, which is crucial for financial tracking and management.

Determine Staff Availability

A7	▼	*fx* =DETERMINE_STAFF_AVAILABILITY(A2:A6, B2:F6)			

	A	B	C	D	E	F
1	Employee	Monday	Tuesday	Wednesday	Thursday	Friday
2	Alice	Available	Unavailable	Available	Unavailable	Available
3	Bob	Unavailable	Available	Available	Available	Unavailable
4	Carol	Available	Available	Unavailable	Available	Available
5	David	Unavailable	Unavailable	Available	Available	Available
6	Emily	Available	Available	Available	Unavailable	Unavailable
7	Alice	Monday, Wednesday, Friday				
8	Bob	Tuesday, Wednesday, Thursday				
9	Carol	Monday, Tuesday, Thursday, Friday				
10	David	Wednesday, Thursday, Friday				
11	Emily	Monday, Tuesday, Wednesday				

Objective: Write a function to determine which days of the week staff members are available based on their schedules.
Sample Data:

Employee	Monday	Tuesday	Wednesday	Thursday	Friday
Alice	Available	Unavailable	Available	Unavailable	Available
Bob	Unavailable	Available	Available	Available	Unavailable
Carol	Available	Available	Unavailable	Available	Available
David	Unavailable	Unavailable	Available	Available	Available
Emily	Available	Available	Available	Unavailable	Unavailable

Learning Outcomes:
- Learn to filter and summarize availability data across multiple days.

- Practice using logical operations to generate structured availability reports.

Code Example:

```
/**
 * Determines the days of the week each staff member is
available.
 *
 * @param {range} employees The range containing employee
names.
 * @param {range} days The range containing availability data
for Monday through Friday.
 * @return {array|string} An array listing each employee with
their available days, or an error message if data is invalid.
 * @customfunction
 */
function DETERMINE_STAFF_AVAILABILITY(employees,
days) {
const results = [];
const weekdays = ['Monday', 'Tuesday', 'Wednesday',
'Thursday', 'Friday'];
for (let i = 0; i < employees.length; i++) {
const availableDays = [];
for (let j = 0; j < days[i].length; j++) {
if (days[i][j] === 'Available') {
availableDays.push(weekdays[j]);
}
}
results.push([employees[i][0], availableDays.join(", ")]);
}
return results.length > 0 ? results : "Invalid or empty data!";
}
```

Steps:

1. Paste the code into a new Apps Script project.
2. Save the changes and return to Google Sheets.
3. Enter the sample data into a grid format from A1:F6.

4. Use the function like =DETERMINE_STAFF_AVAILABILITY(A2:A6, B2:F6).

Expected Result: The function will list each employee along with the days they are available to work, helping in scheduling and workforce management.

Generate Random Alphanumeric String

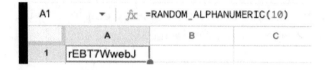

RANDOM_ALPHANUMERIC

(No input data needed, this function generates its own data.)

Objective: Create a custom function that generates a random alphanumeric string of a specified length.

Learning Outcomes:
- Understand how to build custom random string generators.
- Practice working with arrays and strings for character selection.

Code Example:
```
/**
 * Generates a random alphanumeric string of a specified
length.
 *
 * @param {number} length The desired length of the random
string.
 * @return {string} The generated random alphanumeric
string.
 * @customfunction
```

```
*/
function RANDOM_ALPHANUMERIC(length) {
if (typeof length !== 'number' || length <= 0) return "Invalid
length";

const characters =
'ABCDEFGHIJKLMNOPQRSTUVWXYZabcdefghijklmnopqr
stuvwxyz0123456789';
let result = '';
for (let i = 0; i < length; i++) {
result += characters.charAt(Math.floor(Math.random() *
characters.length));
}
return result;
}
```

Steps:
1. Add the code to a new Apps Script project.
2. Save the changes and return to Google Sheets.
3. Use the function with
   =RANDOM_ALPHANUMERIC(10).

Expected Result: The function will return a randomly generated alphanumeric string of 10 characters.

Convert List to Sentence

A2	▾	fx	=LIST_TO_SENTENCE(A1:E1)		
	A	B	C	D	E
1	Apple	Banana	Cherry	Date	Elderberry
2	Apple, Banana, Cherry, Date, and Elderberry.				

LIST_TO_SENTENCE

Apple	Banana	Cherry	Date	Elderberry

Objective: Create a function that converts a range of individual words into a single grammatically correct sentence.

Learning Outcomes:
- Practice string manipulation and array handling to concatenate words.
- Learn conditional logic to handle different list lengths.

Code Example:

```
/**
 * Converts a range of words into a grammatically correct
sentence.
 *
 * @param {range} words The range of words to combine into
a sentence.
 * @return {string} The formatted sentence.
 * @customfunction
 */
function LIST_TO_SENTENCE(words) {
const flatWords = words.flat().filter(word => typeof word
=== 'string' && word.trim() !== '');
const count = flatWords.length;

if (count === 0) return "No words provided!";
if (count === 1) return flatWords[0] + '.';
if (count === 2) return flatWords.join(' and ') + '.';

return flatWords.slice(0, count - 1).join(', ') + ', and ' +
flatWords[count - 1] + '.';
}
```

Steps:
1. Add this code to a new Apps Script project.
2. Save and return to Google Sheets.
3. Enter a list of words in a column, e.g., A1:A5.
4. Use the function like =LIST_TO_SENTENCE(A1:A5).

Expected Result: The function will return a sentence with proper grammatical structure based on the input list length.

Calculate Compound Interest

	A	B	C	D
1	Principal	Rate	Times Compounded	Years
2	1000	5	4	10
3	1643.62			

COMPOUND_INTEREST

Principal	Rate	Times Compounded	Years
1000	5	4	10

Objective: Write a function to calculate compound interest based on principal, rate, and time period.

Learning Outcomes:

- Understand the formula for compound interest calculation.
- Practice using mathematical functions to apply exponential calculations.

Code Example:

```
/**
 * Calculates the compound interest based on principal, rate,
and time period.
 *
 * @param {number} principal The initial amount of money.
 * @param {number} rate The annual interest rate as a
percentage.
 * @param {number} timesCompounded The number of times
interest is compounded per year.
 * @param {number} years The number of years the money is
invested or borrowed for.
 * @return {number} The total amount accumulated after n
years, including interest.
 * @customfunction
 */
```

```
function COMPOUND_INTEREST(principal, rate,
timesCompounded, years) {
 const effectiveRate = rate / 100;
 const accumulatedAmount = principal * Math.pow(1 +
effectiveRate / timesCompounded, timesCompounded *
years);
 return accumulatedAmount.toFixed(2);
}
```

Steps:
1. Paste the code into a new Apps Script project.
2. Save the script and return to Google Sheets.
3. Use the custom function with
   =COMPOUND_INTEREST(1000, 5, 4, 10).

Expected Result: The function will return the accumulated amount after 10 years, assuming an annual interest rate of 5% and quarterly compounding.

Convert Date to Day of the Week

| B1 | ▼ | *fx* =DAY_OF_WEEK(A1) |

	A	B
1	2024-05-22	Wednesday
2	2024-12-25	Wednesday
3	2025-01-01	Wednesday
4	2025-07-04	Friday
5	2026-11-01	Sunday
6		

DAY_OF_WEEK

2024-05-22
2024-12-25
2025-01-01

| 2025-07-04 |
| 2026-11-01 |

Objective: Write a function that converts a date to its corresponding day of the week.

Learning Outcomes:

- Learn how to work with date objects in JavaScript.
- Practice using methods to extract date components and identify the day.

Code Example:

```
/**
 * Converts a date to the corresponding day of the week.
 *
 * @param {date} dateValue The date to convert.
 * @return {string} The name of the day of the week.
 * @customfunction
 */
function DAY_OF_WEEK(dateValue) {
if (!(dateValue instanceof Date)) return "Invalid date";

const days = ['Sunday', 'Monday', 'Tuesday', 'Wednesday',
'Thursday', 'Friday', 'Saturday'];
const dayIndex = dateValue.getDay();
return days[dayIndex];
}
```

Steps:

1. Add this code to a new Apps Script project.
2. Save the changes and return to Google Sheets.
3. Enter a date in a cell, e.g., A1.
4. Use the function like =DAY_OF_WEEK(A1).

Expected Result: The function will return the name of the day of the week corresponding to the given date.

Calculate Weighted Average

| A6 | ▾ | ƒx =WEIGHTED_AVERAGE(A2:A5, B2:B5) |

	A	B	C
1	Value	Weight	
2	80	2	
3	95	1	
4	70	3	
5	85	4	
6	80.50		

Objective: Write a function that calculates the weighted average of a set of values, given their corresponding weights.

Sample Data:

Value	Weight
80	2
95	1
70	3
85	4

Learning Outcomes:

- Understand the concept of calculating weighted averages.
- Learn how to use array manipulation and arithmetic operations.

Code Example:

```
/**
 * Calculates the weighted average of a range of values with
corresponding weights.
 *
 * @param {range} values The range of values.
 * @param {range} weights The range of weights.
 * @return {number|string} The calculated weighted average
or an error message if input data is invalid.
 * @customfunction
 */
function WEIGHTED_AVERAGE(values, weights) {
 if (values.length !== weights.length || values.length === 0)
 return "Invalid data!";
```

```
let weightedSum = 0;
let totalWeight = 0;
for (let i = 0; i < values.length; i++) {
if (typeof values[i][0] === 'number' && typeof weights[i][0]
=== 'number') {
weightedSum += values[i][0] * weights[i][0];
totalWeight += weights[i][0];
}
}
return totalWeight > 0 ? (weightedSum /
totalWeight).toFixed(2) : "Invalid weights!";
}
```

Steps:
1. Paste the code into a new Apps Script project.
2. Save changes and return to Google Sheets.
3. Enter the sample data above into cells A1:B5.
4. Use the function with
   =WEIGHTED_AVERAGE(A2:A5, B2:B5).

Expected Result: The function will return the calculated weighted average of the values based on their weights.

Count Words of Specific Length

B1	▼	*fx* =COUNT_WORDS_BY_LENGTH(A1:A4, 5)	
	A		B
1	This is a sample sentence		2
2	Another example of text		
3	Words of varying length here		
4	Texts with different lengths		

Objective: Write a function that counts words of a specified length within a range of text.

Sample Data:

Text
This is a sample sentence
Another example of text
Words of varying length here

Learning Outcomes:
- Practice string manipulation and regular expressions.
- Learn to count occurrences based on specific criteria.

Code Example:

```
/**
 * Counts words of a specific length in a given range of text.
 *
 * @param {range} data The range containing text to search.
 * @param {number} wordLength The desired word length to count.
 * @return {number|string} The count of words or an error message if input data is invalid.
 * @customfunction
 */
function COUNT_WORDS_BY_LENGTH(data, wordLength) {
if (typeof wordLength !== 'number' || wordLength <= 0) return "Invalid word length!";
  let wordCount = 0;
  data.flat().forEach(text => {
if (typeof text === 'string') {
const matches = text.match(new RegExp(`\\b\\w{${wordLength}}\\b`, 'g'));
  wordCount += matches ? matches.length : 0;
}
});


  return wordCount;
}
```

Steps:
1. Paste the code into a new Apps Script project.
2. Save changes and return to Google Sheets.
3. Enter the sample data into column A1:A5.
4. Use the function like
   =COUNT_WORDS_BY_LENGTH(A1:A5, 5).

Expected Result: The function will return the count of words with a length of 5 in the given range.

Calculate Percentage Distribution of Categories

	A	B	C
1	Fruit	Fruit	42.86%
2	Vegetable	Vegetable	14.29%
3	Fruit	Dairy	28.57%
4	Dairy	Meat	14.29%
5	Fruit		
6	Dairy		
7	Meat		
8	Vegetable		

Objective: Write a function that calculates the percentage distribution of different categories from a list.

Sample Data:

Fruit
Vegetable
Fruit
Dairy
Fruit
Dairy
Meat
Vegetable

Learning Outcomes:
- Learn how to use JavaScript objects for mapping and counting.

- Practice arithmetic operations to calculate percentages.

Code Example:

```
/**
 * Calculates the percentage distribution of categories in a
given range.
 *
 * @param {range} data The range containing the list of
categories.
 * @return {array | string} An array of categories with their
percentage distributions or an error message if input data is
invalid.
 * @customfunction
 */
function CATEGORY_PERCENTAGES(data) {
const total = data.flat().filter(cat => typeof cat ===
'string').length;
if (total === 0) return "No categories found!";

const counts = {};
data.flat().forEach(category => {
if (typeof category === 'string') {
counts[category] = (counts[category] || 0) + 1;
}
});

const result = Object.entries(counts).map(([category, count])
=> [category, ((count / total) * 100).toFixed(2) + '%']);
return result;
}
```

Steps:
1. Paste the code into a new Apps Script project.
2. Save changes and return to Google Sheets.
3. Enter the sample data into column A1:A8.
4. Use the function like
   =CATEGORY_PERCENTAGES(A1:A8).

Expected Result: The function will return an array with each category and its percentage of the total items.

Find the Mode of a Range

B1	▼	fx =FIND_MODE(A1:A8)

	A	B
1	3	7
2	7	
3	3	
4	4	
5	7	
6	7	
7	6	
8	4	

Objective: Create a custom function that finds the mode (most frequently occurring number) in a range of numbers.

Sample Data:

3
7
3
4
7
7
6
4

Learning Outcomes:

- Learn to use objects to count occurrences of each value.
- Understand how to identify the mode from a dataset.

Code Example:

```
/**
 * Finds the mode (most frequently occurring value) in a
range of numbers.
 *
 * @param {range} data The range of numbers to analyze.
 * @return {number | string} The mode value or an error
message if no valid data is found.
 * @customfunction
 */
function FIND_MODE(data) {
const numberCounts = {};
const flatData = data.flat().filter(val => typeof val ===
'number');

if (flatData.length === 0) return "No valid numeric data!";

flatData.forEach(num => numberCounts[num] =
(numberCounts[num] || 0) + 1);

let mode = flatData[0];
let maxCount = numberCounts[mode];

for (let key in numberCounts) {
if (numberCounts[key] > maxCount) {
mode = Number(key);
maxCount = numberCounts[key];
}
}

return mode;
}
```

Steps:

1. Paste this code into a new Apps Script project.
2. Save the changes and return to Google Sheets.
3. Enter the sample data into column A1:A8.
4. Use the function like =FIND_MODE(A1:A8).

Expected Result: The function will return the mode of the given range of numbers.

Find the Longest Word in Each Row

B1	▾	*fx* =LONGEST_WORD_IN_ROWS(A1:A4)	
	A		B
1	This is an interesting exercise		interesting
2	Short sentences count too		sentences
3	Finding the longest word per row		Finding
4	Coding is quite a challenge		challenge

Objective: Create a function that finds the longest word in each row from a range of text data.

Sample Data:

This is an interesting exercise
Short sentences count too
Finding the longest word per row
Coding is quite a challenge

Learning Outcomes:
- Learn to manipulate text data row-wise.
- Understand how to use regular expressions to extract words.

Code Example:

```
/**
* Finds the longest word in each row of text data.
*
* @param {range} data The range of text data.
* @return {array | string} An array of longest words or an
error message if input data is invalid.
* @customfunction
```

```
*/
function LONGEST_WORD_IN_ROWS(data) {
return data.map(row => {
if (typeof row[0] !== 'string') return ["Invalid input"];

const words = row[0].match(/\b\w+\b/g) || [];
const longestWord = words.reduce((longest, current) =>
current.length > longest.length ? current : longest, "");

return [longestWord || "No words found"];
});
}
```

Steps:
1. Paste this code into a new Apps Script project.
2. Save the changes and return to Google Sheets.
3. Enter the sample data into column A1:A4.
4. Use the function like
   =LONGEST_WORD_IN_ROWS(A1:A4).

Expected Result: The function will return an array where each item represents the longest word in its corresponding row.

Check if a Range Contains All Positive Numbers

B1   ▾ | f_x =CHECK_ALL_POSITIVE(A1:A6)

	A	B	C
1	12	Contains Non-Positive	
2	34		
3	-7		
4	45		
5	0		
6	67		

Objective: Write a function to check if all values in a specified range are positive numbers.

Sample Data:

12
34
-7
45
0
67

Learning Outcomes:
- Learn conditional logic to validate numeric data.
- Understand the concept of positive and negative numbers.

Code Example:

```
/**
 * Checks if all values in the range are positive numbers.
 *
 * @param {range} data The range of numbers to check.
 * @return {string} "All Positive" or "Contains Non-Positive"
 depending on the input data.
 * @customfunction
 */
function CHECK_ALL_POSITIVE(data) {
const allPositive = data.flat().every(num => typeof num ===
'number' && num > 0);
 return allPositive ? "All Positive" : "Contains Non-Positive";
}
```

Steps:
1. Add this code into a new Apps Script project.
2. Save and return to Google Sheets.
3. Enter the sample data into column A1:A6.

4. Use the function with
    =CHECK_ALL_POSITIVE(A1:A6).

Expected Result: The function will return "Contains Non-Positive" because there are negative and zero values in the sample data.

Calculate the Standard Deviation of a Range

B1	▾	_fx_ =STANDARD_DEVIATION(A1:A8)

	A	B	C
1	8	2.96	
2	6		
3	10		
4	14		
5	9		
6	11		
7	5		
8	13		

Objective: Write a function to calculate the standard deviation of a set of numerical data.

Sample Data:

8
6
10
14
9
11
5
13

Learning Outcomes:

- Learn to calculate the standard deviation using statistical formulas.
- Practice iterating through numerical data arrays and applying arithmetic operations.

Code Example:

```
/**
 * Calculates the standard deviation of a given range of
numbers.
 *
 * @param {range} data The range of numbers to calculate.
 * @return {number | string} The standard deviation or an
error message if input data is invalid.
 * @customfunction
 */
function STANDARD_DEVIATION(data) {
const numbers = data.flat().filter(val => typeof val ===
'number');
if (numbers.length === 0) return "No valid numeric data!";

const mean = numbers.reduce((sum, val) => sum + val, 0) /
numbers.length;
const variance = numbers.reduce((sum, val) => sum +
Math.pow(val - mean, 2), 0) / numbers.length;
const stdDev = Math.sqrt(variance);

return stdDev.toFixed(2);
}
```

Steps:
1. Paste the code into a new Apps Script project.
2. Save the changes and return to Google Sheets.
3. Enter the sample data into column A1:A8.
4. Use the function with =STANDARD_DEVIATION(A1:A8).

Expected Result: The function will return the standard deviation of the values.

3 : Enhancing Text and Date Operations

Dive into functions specifically designed to manipulate text and date formats. Learn techniques for extracting palindromes, counting specific words, and calculating days until future dates. This chapter helps you handle common text and date-related challenges in Google Sheets using custom functions.

Find Palindromic Words in a Range

B1	▼	*fx* =FIND_PALINDROMES(A1:A6)		
	A	B	C	
1	radar	radar		
2	level	level		
3	palindrome	civic		
4	civic	racecar		
5	racecar			
6	world			

Objective: Create a function to find palindromic words in a given range of text data.
Sample Data:

radar
level
palindrome
civic
racecar
world

Learning Outcomes:
- Understand how to manipulate strings and identify palindromic words.
- Practice looping through arrays and applying conditional logic.

Code Example:
```
/**
 * Finds palindromic words in a given range of text data.
 *
 * @param {range} data The range of words to analyze.
 * @return {array | string} An array of palindromic words or
an error message if input data is invalid.
 * @customfunction
 */
function FIND_PALINDROMES(data) {
function isPalindrome(word) {
const sanitized = word.toLowerCase().replace(/[^a-z]/g, '');
return sanitized === sanitized.split('').reverse().join('');
}

const palindromicWords = data.flat().filter(word => typeof
word === 'string' && isPalindrome(word));

return palindromicWords.length > 0 ?
palindromicWords.map(palindrome => [palindrome]) : "No
palindromic words found!";
}
```

Steps:
1. Paste this code into a new Apps Script project.
2. Save the changes and return to Google Sheets.
3. Enter the sample data into column A1:A6.
4. Use the function like
   =FIND_PALINDROMES(A1:A6).

Expected Result: The function will return an array of palindromic words found in the data.

Find the Maximum and Minimum in Each Row

	A	B	C	D	E
1	Row	Value 1	Value 2	Value 3	Value 4
2	1	12	9	15	8
3	2	22	18	19	20
4	3	5	6	7	4
5	4	11	13	10	14
6	15	8			
7	22	18			
8	7	4			
9	14	10			

Objective: Create a function that returns the maximum and minimum values from each row in a table of numerical data.

Sample Data:

Row	Value 1	Value 2	Value 3	Value 4
1	12	9	15	8
2	22	18	19	20
3	5	6	7	4
4	11	13	10	14

Learning Outcomes:
- Practice extracting minimum and maximum values from rows of numerical data.
- Understand how to iterate through a two-dimensional array and apply conditional logic.

Code Example:

```
/**
 * Finds the maximum and minimum values for each row in a
table of numerical data.
 *
 * @param {range} data The table of numerical data.
 * @return {array | string} An array of maximum and
minimum values for each row, or an error message if input
data is invalid.
 * @customfunction
```

```
*/
function MAX_AND_MIN_IN_ROWS(data) {
return data.map(row => {
const numbers = row.filter(val => typeof val === 'number');
if (numbers.length === 0) return ["No valid numeric data!"];

return [Math.max(...numbers), Math.min(...numbers)];
});
}
```

Steps:
1. Paste the code into a new Apps Script project.
2. Save the changes and return to Google Sheets.
3. Enter the sample data into range A1:E5.
4. Use the function like
   =MAX_AND_MIN_IN_ROWS(B2:E5).

Expected Result: The function will return an array where each item contains the maximum and minimum values from each row.

Sum Numbers by Category

C1	▾	ƒx	=SUM_BY_CATEGORY(A2:A8, B2:B8)	

	A	B	C	D
1	Category	Amount	Food	95
2	Food	15	Travel	35
3	Travel	25	Shopping	60
4	Food	30		
5	Shopping	40		
6	Travel	10		
7	Shopping	20		
8	Food	50		

Objective: Create a function to calculate the total sum of numbers in each category provided in two columns.

Sample Data:

Category	Amount

Food	15
Travel	25
Food	30
Shopping	40
Travel	10
Shopping	20
Food	50

Learning Outcomes:
- Practice grouping and summing data by categories using objects.
- Understand how to map sums to their corresponding categories.

Code Example:

```
/**
 * Sums numbers for each category specified in the input data.
 *
 * @param {range} categories The range containing categories.
 * @param {range} amounts The range containing amounts
corresponding to each category.
 * @return {array | string} An array with categories and their
total sums, or an error message if input data is invalid.
 * @customfunction
 */
function SUM_BY_CATEGORY(categories, amounts) {
const sums = {};

for (let i = 0; i < categories.length; i++) {
const category = categories[i][0];
const amount = amounts[i][0];

if (typeof category === 'string' && typeof amount ===
'number') {
sums[category] = (sums[category] || 0) + amount;
```

```
    }
}

const result = Object.entries(sums).map(([category, total]) =>
[category, total]);
    return result.length > 0 ? result : "No valid data!";
}
```

Steps:
1. Paste the code into a new Apps Script project.
2. Save the changes and return to Google Sheets.
3. Enter the sample data into columns A1:B8.
4. Use the function like =SUM_BY_CATEGORY(A2:A8, B2:B8).

Expected Result: The function will return an array with each category and its total amount.

Find Rows with Missing Data

	A	B	C	D
	D1	▾	*fx* =FIND_MISSING_ROWS(A2:C7)	
1	Name	Age	Address	2
2	John	29		4
3	Sarah	32	Maple Street	6
4	Michael		Oak Avenue	7
5	Linda	45	Elm Street	
6	Andrew	50		
7		33	Birch Avenue	

Objective: Create a function that identifies rows containing empty cells.

Sample Data:

Name	Age	Address
John	29	
Sarah	32	Maple Street
Michael		Oak Avenue

Linda	45	Elm Street
Andrew	50	
	33	Birch Avenue

Learning Outcomes:
- Learn to identify missing or incomplete data in rows.
- Practice iterating through rows to find empty cells.

Code Example:

```
/**
* Finds rows that contain empty cells in the provided range.
*
* @param {range} data The table to analyze.
* @return {array | string} An array with the row numbers of
rows containing missing data, or an error message if no
missing data is found.
* @customfunction
*/
function FIND_MISSING_ROWS(data) {
const missingRows = [];
for (let i = 0; i < data.length; i++) {
if (data[i].some(cell => cell === "" || cell === null || cell
=== undefined)) {
missingRows.push([i + 2]);
}
}
return missingRows.length > 0 ? missingRows : "No missing
data!";
}
```

Steps:
1. Paste the code into a new Apps Script project.
2. Save the changes and return to Google Sheets.
3. Enter the sample data into range A1:C7.
4. Use the function like
   =FIND_MISSING_ROWS(A2:C7).

Expected Result: The function will return an array with row numbers where there are missing values.

Identify Duplicate Text Strings

B1	▾	fx =FIND_DUPLICATE_TEXTS(A1:A8)	
	A	B	C
1	Apple	Apple	2
2	Banana	Banana	2
3	Apple	Grape	2
4	Cherry		
5	Banana		
6	Grape		
7	Grape		
8	Orange		

Objective: Create a function that identifies duplicate text strings within a range and lists them.

Sample Data:

Apple
Banana
Apple
Cherry
Banana
Grape
Grape
Orange

Learning Outcomes:
- Learn how to identify duplicates in a range of text strings.
- Understand mapping counts to detect and list duplicates.

Code Example:

/**
 * Identifies duplicate text strings in the specified range.

```
*
* @param {range} data The range containing text strings.
* @return {array | string} An array with duplicate text strings
and their counts, or an error message if no duplicates are
found.
* @customfunction
*/
function FIND_DUPLICATE_TEXTS(data) {
const counts = {};
const duplicates = [];
data.flat().forEach(text => {
if (typeof text === 'string' && text.trim()) {
counts[text] = (counts[text] || 0) + 1;
}
});
for (let text in counts) {
if (counts[text] > 1) {
duplicates.push([text, counts[text]]);
}
}
return duplicates.length > 0 ? duplicates : "No duplicates
found!";
}
```

Steps:

1. Add the code into a new Apps Script project.
2. Save the changes and return to Google Sheets.
3. Enter the sample data into column A1:A8.
4. Use the function like
    =FIND_DUPLICATE_TEXTS(A1:A8).

Expected Result: The function will return an array listing the
duplicate text strings and their occurrence counts.

Calculate Total Sales per Product

D1	▼	*fx* =TOTAL_SALES_PER_PRODUCT(A2:A7, B2:B7, C2:C7)			
	A	B	C	D	E
1	Product	Quantity	Unit Price	Laptop	2700.00
2	Laptop	2	900	Phone	2100.00
3	Phone	5	300	Tablet	1800.00
4	Laptop	1	900		
5	Tablet	3	450		
6	Phone	2	300		
7	Tablet	1	450		

Objective: Write a function to calculate the total sales for each product given sales data.

Sample Data:

Product	Quantity	Unit Price
Laptop	2	900
Phone	5	300
Laptop	1	900
Tablet	3	450
Phone	2	300
Tablet	1	450

Learning Outcomes:
- Learn to group and sum data for each product.
- Understand the importance of iterating through arrays for data aggregation.

Code Example:

```
/**
 * Calculates total sales per product.
 *
 * @param {range} products The range of product names.
 * @param {range} quantities The range of quantities sold.
 * @param {range} prices The range of unit prices.
 * @return {array | string} An array with product names and
their total sales, or an error message if input data is invalid.
 * @customfunction
```

```
*/
function TOTAL_SALES_PER_PRODUCT(products,
quantities, prices) {
 const sales = {};
 for (let i = 0; i < products.length; i++) {
 const product = products[i][0];
 const quantity = quantities[i][0];
 const price = prices[i][0];
 if (typeof product === 'string' && typeof quantity ===
'number' && typeof price === 'number') {
 sales[product] = (sales[product] || 0) + quantity * price;
 }
 }
 const result = Object.entries(sales).map(([product, total]) =>
[product, total.toFixed(2)]);
 return result.length > 0 ? result : "Invalid or empty data!";
}
```

Steps:

1. Paste this code into a new Apps Script project.
2. Save the changes and return to Google Sheets.
3. Enter the sample data into columns A1:C7.
4. Use the function like
   =TOTAL_SALES_PER_PRODUCT(A2:A7, B2:B7,
   C2:C7).

Expected Result: The function will return an array showing the total sales for each product.

Count Rows Matching Criteria

C1   ▾   *fx* =COUNT_ROWS_BY_STATUS(B2:B7, "Active")

	A	B	C	D
1	Name	Status	4	
2	Sarah	Active		
3	John	Inactive		
4	Emily	Active		
5	Michael	Active		
6	Linda	Inactive		
7	Andrew	Active		

Objective: Write a function to count the number of rows where a specific column value matches a given criteria.

Sample Data:

Name	Status
Sarah	Active
John	Inactive
Emily	Active
Michael	Active
Linda	Inactive
Andrew	Active

Learning Outcomes:
- Learn to filter rows based on specific criteria.
- Understand how to work with logical conditions to count matches.

Code Example:

```
/**
 * Counts rows matching a specific value in a column.
 *
 * @param {range} data The range to analyze.
 * @param {string} status The value to match in the specified column.
 * @return {number | string} The count of matching rows or an error message if no valid data is found.
 * @customfunction
 */
function COUNT_ROWS_BY_STATUS(data, status) {
 if (typeof status !== 'string') return "Invalid status";
 const count = data.flat().filter(item => item === status).length;
 return count > 0 ? count : "No matching rows found";
}
```

Steps:

1. Paste the code into a new Apps Script project.
2. Save the changes and return to Google Sheets.
3. Enter the sample data into columns A1:B7.
4. Use the function like
   =COUNT_ROWS_BY_STATUS(B2:B7, "Active").

Expected Result: The function will return the count of rows where "Active" is the value in the Status column.

Identify Unique Values in a Column

B1	▼	*fx* =UNIQUE_VALUES(A2:A8)

	A	B	C
1	Category	Sports	
2	Sports	News	
3	News	Travel	
4	Travel	Technology	
5	Sports		
6	Technology		
7	News		
8	Travel		

Objective: Write a function that returns unique values from a specified column.

Sample Data:

Category
Sports
News
Travel
Sports
Technology
News
Travel

Learning Outcomes:
- Learn to identify and collect unique values from a dataset.
- Understand how to use sets to filter unique items efficiently.

Code Example:
```
/**
 * Returns unique values from a specified column.
 *
 * @param {range} data The range to analyze.
 * @return {array | string} An array of unique values or an
error message if no valid data is found.
 * @customfunction
 */
function UNIQUE_VALUES(data) {
const uniqueSet = new Set(data.flat().filter(val => typeof val
=== 'string' && val.trim() !== ""));
const result = Array.from(uniqueSet).map(val => [val]);
return result.length > 0 ? result : "No valid data!";
}
```

Steps:
1. Paste the code into a new Apps Script project.
2. Save the changes and return to Google Sheets.
3. Enter the sample data into column A1:A8.
4. Use the function like =UNIQUE_VALUES(A2:A8).

Expected Result: The function will return an array containing unique values from the Category column.

Calculate Cumulative Sum by Date

C1   ▾   ƒx =CUMULATIVE_SUM_BY_DATE(A2:A7, B2:B7)

	A	B	C	D
1	Date	Value	2024-01-01	10
2	2024-01-01	10	2024-01-02	30
3	2024-01-02	20	2024-01-03	45
4	2024-01-03	15	2024-01-04	75
5	2024-01-04	30	2024-01-05	100
6	2024-01-05	25	2024-01-06	140
7	2024-01-06	40		

Objective: Write a function to calculate the cumulative sum of values based on dates.

Sample Data:

Date	Value
2024-01-01	10
2024-01-02	20
2024-01-03	15
2024-01-04	30
2024-01-05	25
2024-01-06	40

Learning Outcomes:
- Learn how to handle and parse date objects.
- Understand how to iterate over sorted dates and calculate cumulative sums.

Code Example:

```
/**
* Calculates the cumulative sum of values grouped by date.
*
* @param {range} dates The range containing the dates.
* @param {range} values The range containing the values
associated with each date.
* @return {array | string} An array with dates and their
cumulative sums, or an error message if input data is invalid.
```

```
 * @customfunction
 */
function CUMULATIVE_SUM_BY_DATE(dates, values) {
 const data = dates.map((date, index) => ({ date: new
Date(date[0]), value: values[index][0] })).filter(item =>
!isNaN(item.date) && typeof item.value === 'number');
 if (data.length === 0) return "Invalid data or empty range!";
 data.sort((a, b) => a.date - b.date);
 let cumulativeSum = 0;
let result = data.map(item => {
 cumulativeSum += item.value;
 return [item.date.toISOString().split('T')[0], cumulativeSum];
 });
 return result;
}
```

Steps:

1. Paste the code into a new Apps Script project.
2. Save the changes and return to Google Sheets.
3. Enter the sample data into columns A1:B7.
4. Use the function like
   =CUMULATIVE_SUM_BY_DATE(A2:A7, B2:B7).

Expected Result: The function will return an array with each date and its corresponding cumulative sum.

List Employees Above a Certain Age

fx =EMPLOYEES_ABOVE_AGE(A2:A7, B2:B7, 30)

	A	B	C	D
1	Name	Age	Michael	
2	Sarah	28	Emily	
3	Michael	35	Linda	
4	Emily	42	John	
5	Linda	31		
6	Andrew	29		
7	John	50		

Objective: Write a function to list employees who are above a specified age.

Sample Data:

Name	Age
Sarah	28
Michael	35
Emily	42
Linda	31
Andrew	29
John	50

Learning Outcomes:
- Learn to apply conditional logic to numerical columns.
- Practice filtering data by age criteria.

Code Example:

```
/**
 * Lists employees above a specified age.
 *
 * @param {range} names The range containing employee names.
 * @param {range} ages The range containing corresponding ages.
 * @param {number} minAge The minimum age to include in the result.
```

* @return {array | string} An array of names who are above the specified age, or an error message if no valid data is found.
* @customfunction
*/

```
function EMPLOYEES_ABOVE_AGE(names, ages, minAge) {
  if (typeof minAge !== 'number' || minAge <= 0) return
"Invalid age parameter!";
  const result = [];
for (let i = 0; i < names.length; i++) {
  const name = names[i][0];
  const age = ages[i][0];
  if (typeof name === 'string' && typeof age === 'number' &&
age > minAge) {
  result.push([name]);
  }
  }
  return result.length > 0 ? result : "No employees found above
the specified age!";
}
```

Steps:

1. Paste this code into a new Apps Script project.
2. Save the changes and return to Google Sheets.
3. Enter the sample data into columns A1:B7.
4. Use the function like
   =EMPLOYEES_ABOVE_AGE(A2:A7, B2:B7, 30).

Expected Result: The function will return an array containing names of employees who are above the specified age of 30.

Calculate Average Rating per Category

	A	B	C	D	E
1	Category	Item	Rating		
2	Electronics	Phone	4	Electronics	4.33
3	Clothing	Shirt	3	Clothing	3.50
4	Electronics	Laptop	5	Furniture	4.00
5	Clothing	Pants	4		
6	Furniture	Chair	3		
7	Electronics	Tablet	4		
8	Furniture	Table	5		

Objective: Write a function to calculate the average rating of different items per category.

Sample Data:

Category	Item	Rating
Electronics	Phone	4
Clothing	Shirt	3
Electronics	Laptop	5
Clothing	Pants	4
Furniture	Chair	3
Electronics	Tablet	4
Furniture	Table	5

Learning Outcomes:
- Learn to group items by category.
- Practice calculating averages by aggregating ratings.

Code Example:
```
/**
* Calculates the average rating per category.
*
* @param {range} categories The range containing categories.
* @param {range} ratings The range containing the ratings.
* @return {array | string} An array of categories with their
average ratings, or an error message if no valid data is found.
* @customfunction
*/
```

```
function AVERAGE_RATING_BY_CATEGORY(categories,
ratings) {
 const totals = {};
 const counts = {};
 for (let i = 0; i < categories.length; i++) {
 const category = categories[i][0];
 const rating = ratings[i][0];
 if (typeof category === 'string' && typeof rating ===
'number') {
 totals[category] = (totals[category] || 0) + rating;
 counts[category] = (counts[category] || 0) + 1;
 }
 }
 const result = Object.entries(totals).map(([category, total]) =>
[category, (total / counts[category]).toFixed(2)]);
 return result.length > 0 ? result : "No valid data!";
}
```

Steps:

1. Paste the code into a new Apps Script project.
2. Save the changes and return to Google Sheets.
3. Enter the sample data into columns A1:C8.
4. Use the function like
   =AVERAGE_RATING_BY_CATEGORY(A2:A8,
   C2:C8).

Expected Result: The function will return an array of each category with its calculated average rating.

Calculate Year-over-Year Growth

C2	▾	fx =YEAR_OVER_YEAR_GROWTH(A2:A6, B2:B6)		
	A	B	C	D
1	Year	Sales		
2	2021	500	Year	Growth %
3	2022	600	2022	20.00%
4	2023	720	2023	20.00%
5	2024	850	2024	18.06%
6	2025	930	2025	9.41%

Objective: Write a function to calculate the year-over-year growth of sales data.

Sample Data:

Year	Sales
2021	500
2022	600
2023	720
2024	850
2025	930

Learning Outcomes:
- Learn how to calculate growth rates between consecutive years.
- Practice conditional logic for identifying and handling data gaps.

Code Example:

```
/**
 * Calculates year-over-year growth of sales data.
 *
 * @param {range} years The range containing the years.
 * @param {range} sales The range containing sales data.
 * @return {array|string} An array with years and their
corresponding growth rates, or an error message if input data
is invalid.
 * @customfunction
 */
function YEAR_OVER_YEAR_GROWTH(years, sales) {
  const result = [["Year", "Growth %"]];
  for (let i = 1; i < years.length; i++) {
    const year = years[i][0];
    const prevSales = sales[i - 1][0];
    const currSales = sales[i][0];
    if (typeof year !== 'number' || typeof prevSales !== 'number'
|| typeof currSales !== 'number') {
```

```
    return "Invalid data!";
    }
    const growthRate = ((currSales - prevSales) / prevSales) *
    100;
    result.push([year, growthRate.toFixed(2) + "%"]);
    }
    return result.length > 1 ? result : "Not enough data to
    calculate growth!";
}
```

Steps:

1. Paste the code into a new Apps Script project.
2. Save the changes and return to Google Sheets.
3. Enter the sample data into columns A1:B6.
4. Use the function like
   =YEAR_OVER_YEAR_GROWTH(A2:A6, B2:B6).

Expected Result: The function will return an array showing the growth percentage for each year after the first.

4 : Custom Solutions for Business Scenarios

Tailor your Google Sheets to solve real-world business problems. This chapter focuses on creating custom functions that solve typical business needs such as generating reports, calculating sales metrics, and assessing project timelines. Each function is designed to be directly applicable in business contexts.

Find Overlapping Date Ranges

C2		fx =FIND_OVERLAPPING_DATES(A2:A6, B2:B6)		
	A	B	C	D
1	Start Date	End Date		
2	2024-01-01	2024-01-10	Range 1 overlaps with Range 2	
3	2024-01-05	2024-01-15	Range 3 overlaps with Range 4	
4	2024-02-01	2024-02-05		
5	2024-02-03	2024-02-08		
6	2024-03-01	2024-03-10		

Objective: Write a function that identifies overlapping date ranges given two columns with start and end dates.

Sample Data:

Learning Outcomes:

- Understand how to compare date objects.
- Learn to identify overlapping ranges based on start and end points.

Code Example:

```
/**
 * Finds overlapping date ranges given start and end dates.
 *
 * @param {range} startDates The range containing start dates.
 * @param {range} endDates The range containing end dates.
 * @return {array | string} An array with overlapping date
 ranges or an error message if input data is invalid.
 * @customfunction
```

```
*/
function FIND_OVERLAPPING_DATES(startDates,
endDates) {
 const ranges = startDates.map((start, index) => ({ start: new
Date(start[0]), end: new Date(endDates[index][0]) }));
 const overlaps = [];
for (let i = 0; i < ranges.length; i++) {
for (let j = i + 1; j < ranges.length; j++) {
if (ranges[i].start <= ranges[j].end && ranges[i].end >=
ranges[j].start) {
overlaps.push([`Range ${i + 1} overlaps with Range ${j +
1}`]);
}
}
}
 return overlaps.length > 0 ? overlaps : "No overlapping dates
found!";
}
```

Steps:

1. Paste the code into a new Apps Script project.
2. Save the changes and return to Google Sheets.
3. Enter the sample data into columns A1:B6.
4. Use the function like
   =FIND_OVERLAPPING_DATES(A2:A6, B2:B6).

Expected Result: The function will return a list of
overlapping date ranges.

Generate Full Names from First and Last Names

	A	B	C	
1	First Name	Last Name		
2	John	Doe	John Doe	
3	Sarah	Smith	Sarah Smith	
4	Michael	Johnson	Michael Johnson	
5	Emily	Brown	Emily Brown	
6	Andrew	Wilson	Andrew Wilson	

C2 ▾ *fx* =GENERATE_FULL_NAMES(A2:A6, B2:B6)

Objective: Write a function that combines first and last names into full names.

Sample Data:

First Name	Last Name
John	Doe
Sarah	Smith
Michael	Johnson
Emily	Brown
Andrew	Wilson

Learning Outcomes:
- Learn to manipulate and concatenate text strings.
- Understand how to handle empty or null values when combining strings.

Code Example:

```
/**
* Combines first and last names to generate full names.
*
* @param {range} firstNames The range containing first names.
* @param {range} lastNames The range containing last names.
```

```
 * @return {array | string} An array with the generated full
names or an error message if input data is invalid.
 * @customfunction
 */
function GENERATE_FULL_NAMES(firstNames, lastNames)
{
 const result = [];
for (let i = 0; i < firstNames.length; i++) {
 const firstName = firstNames[i][0];
 const lastName = lastNames[i][0];
 if (typeof firstName === 'string' && typeof lastName ===
'string') {
 result.push([firstName.trim() + " " + lastName.trim()]);
 } else {
 result.push(["Invalid input"]);
 }
 }
 return result.length > 0 ? result : "No valid data!";
}
```

Steps:

1. Paste the code into a new Apps Script project.
2. Save the changes and return to Google Sheets.
3. Enter the sample data into columns A1:B6.
4. Use the function like
   =GENERATE_FULL_NAMES(A2:A6, B2:B6).

Expected Result: The function will return an array with full
names created from the provided first and last names.

Longest Consecutive Streak of Positive Sales

C2	▼	fx =LONGEST_POSITIVE_STREAK(B2:B10)	

	A	B	C
1	Day	Sales	
2	1	50	3
3	2	30	
4	3	-10	
5	4	20	
6	5	40	
7	6	50	
8	7	-15	
9	8	10	
10	9	30	

Objective: Write a function to find the longest consecutive streak of positive sales from a given list.

Sample Data:

Day	Sales
1	50
2	30
3	-10
4	20
5	40
6	50
7	-15
8	10
9	30

Learning Outcomes:
- Understand how to identify consecutive patterns in numerical data.
- Practice conditional logic to determine streak lengths.

Code Example:

```
/**
 * Finds the longest consecutive streak of positive sales.
 *
 * @param {range} sales The range of daily sales data.
 * @return {number | string} The length of the longest positive
sales streak or an error message if input data is invalid.
 * @customfunction
 */
function LONGEST_POSITIVE_STREAK(sales) {
let maxStreak = 0;
let currentStreak = 0;
for (let i = 0; i < sales.length; i++) {
const sale = sales[i][0];
if (typeof sale === 'number' && sale > 0) {
currentStreak++;
} else {
maxStreak = Math.max(maxStreak, currentStreak);
currentStreak = 0;
}
}
maxStreak = Math.max(maxStreak, currentStreak);
return maxStreak > 0 ? maxStreak : "No positive streak
found!";
}
```

Steps:

1. Paste the code into a new Apps Script project.
2. Save the changes and return to Google Sheets.
3. Enter the sample data into columns A1:B10.
4. Use the function like
   =LONGEST_POSITIVE_STREAK(B2:B10).

Expected Result: The function will return the longest streak of consecutive positive sales.

Calculate Total Expenses by Month

C2	▾	ƒx =TOTAL_EXPENSES_BY_MONTH(A2:A8, B2:B8)		
	A	B	C	D
1	Date	Expense		
2	2024-01-05	200	2024-01	350
3	2024-01-15	150	2024-02	320
4	2024-02-10	220	2024-03	440
5	2024-02-25	100		
6	2024-03-01	180		
7	2024-03-15	90		
8	2024-03-30	170		

Objective: Create a function to calculate the total expenses per month based on a given table with date and expense data.

Sample Data:

Date	Expense
2024-01-05	200
2024-01-15	150
2024-02-10	220
2024-02-25	100
2024-03-01	180
2024-03-15	90
2024-03-30	170

Learning Outcomes:
- Learn to group and aggregate expenses by month using date components.
- Understand how to extract and manipulate date information.

Code Example:

```
/**
* Calculates the total expenses for each month.
*
* @param {range} dates The range containing the dates.
```

* @param {range} expenses The range containing the corresponding expenses.
 * @return {array | string} An array of months with their total expenses, or an error message if input data is invalid.
 * @customfunction
 */

```
function TOTAL_EXPENSES_BY_MONTH(dates, expenses) {
const monthlyExpenses = {};
for (let i = 0; i < dates.length; i++) {
const date = new Date(dates[i][0]);
const expense = expenses[i][0];
if (!isNaN(date) && typeof expense === 'number') {
const monthYear = date.toISOString().slice(0, 7);
monthlyExpenses[monthYear] =
(monthlyExpenses[monthYear] || 0) + expense;
}
}
const result =
Object.entries(monthlyExpenses).map(([month, total]) =>
[month, total]);
return result.length > 0 ? result : "No valid data found!";
}
```

Steps:

1. Paste the code into a new Apps Script project.
2. Save the changes and return to Google Sheets.
3. Enter the sample data into columns A1:B8.
4. Use the function like
   =TOTAL_EXPENSES_BY_MONTH(A2:A8, B2:B8).

Expected Result: The function will return an array of months and their total expenses.

Identify Top-N Performers by Score

	A	B	C	D
		fx =TOP_N_PERFORMERS(A2:A8, B2:B8, 3)		

C2	▼	fx =TOP_N_PERFORMERS(A2:A8, B2:B8, 3)		
	A	B	C	D
1	Name	Score		
2	Sarah	90	Karen	95
3	Michael	85	Emily	92
4	Emily	92	Sarah	90
5	John	88		
6	Andrew	75		
7	Linda	80		
8	Karen	95		

Objective: Create a function to identify the top-N performers based on scores.

Sample Data:

Name	Score
Sarah	90
Michael	85
Emily	92
John	88
Andrew	75
Linda	80
Karen	95

Learning Outcomes:
- Learn to sort and filter data based on numerical scores.
- Practice conditional logic to identify top performers.

Code Example:
```
/**
 * Identifies the top-N performers based on scores.
 *
 * @param {range} names The range containing the names.
 * @param {range} scores The range containing the scores.
```

```
 * @param {number} n The number of top performers to
return.
 * @return {array | string} An array of top-N performers and
their scores, or an error message if input data is invalid.
 * @customfunction
 */
function TOP_N_PERFORMERS(names, scores, n) {
 if (typeof n !== 'number' || n <= 0) return "Invalid value for
N";
 const data = names.map((name, index) => ({ name: name[0],
score: scores[index][0] }))
 .filter(item => typeof item.name === 'string' && typeof
item.score === 'number')
 .sort((a, b) => b.score - a.score);
 const result = data.slice(0, n).map(item => [item.name,
item.score]);
 return result.length > 0 ? result : "Not enough data!";
}
```

Steps:

1. Paste the code into a new Apps Script project.
2. Save the changes and return to Google Sheets.
3. Enter the sample data into columns A1:B8.
4. Use the function like =TOP_N_PERFORMERS(A2:A8, B2:B8, 3).

Expected Result: The function will return an array containing the top 3 performers and their scores.

Count Items by Category

	A	B	C	D
1	Category	Item		
2	Furniture	Chair	Furniture	3
3	Furniture	Table	Electronics	2
4	Electronics	Phone	Grocery	2
5	Furniture	Sofa		
6	Electronics	Laptop		
7	Grocery	Apple		
8	Grocery	Banana		

Objective: Write a function to count the total number of items per category.

Sample Data:

Category	Item
Furniture	Chair
Furniture	Table
Electronics	Phone
Furniture	Sofa
Electronics	Laptop
Grocery	Apple
Grocery	Banana

Learning Outcomes:
- Learn how to group items by category.
- Practice counting items using an object for mapping.

Code Example:
```
/**
* Counts the total number of items per category.
*
* @param {range} categories The range containing the
category names.
```

* @return {array | string} An array with the categories and their respective counts, or an error message if input data is invalid.
* @customfunction
*/

```
function COUNT_ITEMS_BY_CATEGORY(categories) {
const counts = {};
categories.flat().forEach(category => {
if (typeof category === 'string' && category.trim() !== '') {
counts[category] = (counts[category] || 0) + 1;
}
});
const result = Object.entries(counts).map(([category, count])
=> [category, count]);
return result.length > 0 ? result : "No valid categories
found!";
}
```

Steps:
1. Paste the code into a new Apps Script project.
2. Save the changes and return to Google Sheets.
3. Enter the sample data into columns A1:B8.
4. Use the function like
   =COUNT_ITEMS_BY_CATEGORY(A2:A8).

Expected Result: The function will return an array showing the count of items for each category.

Sum Revenue by Product Type

D2	▾	fx	=TOTAL_REVENUE_BY_PRODUCT_TYPE(A2:A7, B2:B7, C2:C7)	
	A	B	C	D	E
1	Product Type	Units Sold	Price per Unit		
2	Laptop	4	800	Laptop	4800.00
3	Phone	10	400	Phone	7200.00
4	Tablet	6	300	Tablet	3300.00
5	Laptop	2	800		
6	Phone	8	400		
7	Tablet	5	300		

Objective: Write a function to calculate the total revenue for each product type, given sales data.

Sample Data:

Product Type	Units Sold	Price per Unit
Laptop	4	800
Phone	10	400
Tablet	6	300
Laptop	2	800
Phone	8	400
Tablet	5	300

Learning Outcomes:
- Learn how to group data by product type.
- Practice summing values using the quantity and unit price.

Code Example:

```
/**
 * Calculates the total revenue by product type.
 *
 * @param {range} types The range containing product types.
 * @param {range} unitsSold The range containing units sold
 * for each product type.
 * @param {range} prices The range containing the unit price
 * for each product type.
 * @return {array | string} An array with product types and
 * their total revenue, or an error message if input data is
 * invalid.
 * @customfunction
 */
function TOTAL_REVENUE_BY_PRODUCT_TYPE(types,
unitsSold, prices) {
  const revenue = {};
  for (let i = 0; i < types.length; i++) {
    const type = types[i][0];
    const units = unitsSold[i][0];
```

```
const price = prices[i][0];
if (typeof type === 'string' && typeof units === 'number' &&
typeof price === 'number') {
revenue[type] = (revenue[type] || 0) + units * price;
}
}
const result = Object.entries(revenue).map(([type, total]) =>
[type, total.toFixed(2)]);
 return result.length > 0 ? result : "Invalid or empty data!";
}
```

Steps:

1. Paste this code into a new Apps Script project.
2. Save the changes and return to Google Sheets.
3. Enter the sample data into columns A1:C7.
4. Use the function like
    =TOTAL_REVENUE_BY_PRODUCT_TYPE(A2:A7,
    B2:B7, C2:C7).

Expected Result: The function will return an array of product types and their total revenue.

List Unique Customers by Region

C2	▾	fx =UNIQUE_CUSTOMERS_BY_REGION(A2:A9, B2:B9)		
	A	B	C	D
1	Region	Customer		
2	North	Alice	North	Alice, David, George
3	South	Bob	South	Bob, Frank
4	East	Carol	East	Carol, Alice
5	North	David	West	Eve
6	East	Alice		
7	West	Eve		
8	South	Frank		
9	North	George		

Objective: Write a function that lists unique customer names grouped by region.

Sample Data:

Region	Customer

North	Alice
South	Bob
East	Carol
North	David
East	Alice
West	Eve
South	Frank
North	George

Learning Outcomes:
- Learn how to identify unique customer names within each region.
- Practice working with sets to ensure uniqueness.

Code Example:

```
/**
 * Lists unique customer names grouped by region.
 *
 * @param {range} regions The range containing region
names.
 * @param {range} customers The range containing customer
names.
 * @return {array | string} An array with regions and their
unique customers, or an error message if input data is
invalid.
 * @customfunction
 */
function UNIQUE_CUSTOMERS_BY_REGION(regions,
customers) {
 const regionMap = {};
for (let i = 0; i < regions.length; i++) {
 const region = regions[i][0];
 const customer = customers[i][0];
 if (typeof region === 'string' && typeof customer ===
'string') {
```

```
if (!regionMap[region]) regionMap[region] = new Set();
regionMap[region].add(customer);
}
}
const result = Object.entries(regionMap).map(([region,
customerSet]) => [region, Array.from(customerSet).join(', ')]);
return result.length > 0 ? result : "No valid data!";
}
```

Steps:

1. Paste the code into a new Apps Script project.
2. Save the changes and return to Google Sheets.
3. Enter the sample data into columns A1:B9.
4. Use the function like
   =UNIQUE_CUSTOMERS_BY_REGION(A2:A9,
   B2:B9).

Expected Result: The function will return an array listing each region and its unique customer names.

First and Last Transaction Date per Customer

C2	▾	ƒx =FIRST_LAST_TRANSACTION_DATE(A2:A8, B2:B8)		
	A	B	C	D	E
1	Customer	Transaction Date			
2	Alice	2024-01-05	Alice	2024-01-05	2024-03-15
3	Bob	2024-02-10	Bob	2024-02-10	2024-03-05
4	Alice	2024-03-15	Carol	2024-01-20	2024-03-25
5	Carol	2024-01-20			
6	Bob	2024-03-05			
7	Carol	2024-03-25			
8	Alice	2024-02-10			

Objective: Write a function to identify the first and last transaction date per customer.

Sample Data:

Customer	Transaction Date
Alice	2024-01-05
Bob	2024-02-10

Alice	2024-03-15
Carol	2024-01-20
Bob	2024-03-05
Carol	2024-03-25
Alice	2024-02-10

Learning Outcomes:
- Understand how to work with date objects in JavaScript.
- Practice finding and grouping the earliest and latest dates for each customer.

Code Example:

```
/**
* Identifies the first and last transaction date for each customer.
*
* @param {range} customers The range containing customer names.
* @param {range} dates The range containing transaction dates.
* @return {array | string} An array with customer names, first date, and last date, or an error message if input data is invalid.
* @customfunction
*/
function FIRST_LAST_TRANSACTION_DATE(customers, dates) {
const transactions = {};
for (let i = 0; i < customers.length; i++) {
const customer = customers[i][0];
const date = new Date(dates[i][0]);
if (typeof customer === 'string' && !isNaN(date)) {
if (!transactions[customer]) {
transactions[customer] = { first: date, last: date };
} else {
```

transactions[customer].first = transactions[customer].first >
date ? date : transactions[customer].first;
transactions[customer].last = transactions[customer].last <
date ? date : transactions[customer].last;

```
    }
  }
}
const result = Object.entries(transactions).map(([customer,
range]) => [
customer, range.first.toISOString().split('T')[0],
range.last.toISOString().split('T')[0]
]);
return result.length > 0 ? result : "Invalid or no data!";
}
```

Steps:
1. Paste the code into a new Apps Script project.
2. Save the changes and return to Google Sheets.
3. Enter the sample data into columns A1:B8.
4. Use the function like
   =FIRST_LAST_TRANSACTION_DATE(A2:A8,
   B2:B8).

Expected Result: The function will return an array listing
each customer with their first and last transaction dates.

List Top-N Customers by Purchase Count

C2   ▾   _fx_ =TOP_N_CUSTOMERS_BY_PURCHASE_COUNT(A2:A8, B2:B8, 3)

	A	B	C	D	E
1	Customer	Purchase Count			
2	Alice	5	George	8	
3	Bob	3	Frank	7	
4	Carol	6	Carol	6	
5	David	4			
6	Eve	2			
7	Frank	7			
8	George	8			

Objective: Write a function to identify the top-N customers
based on their purchase count.
Sample Data:

Customer	Purchase Count
Alice	5
Bob	3
Carol	6
David	4
Eve	2
Frank	7
George	8

Learning Outcomes:
- Learn to sort and filter data by purchase count.
- Practice conditional logic to identify the top-N customers.

Code Example:

```
/**
 * Identifies the top-N customers based on purchase count.
 *
 * @param {range} customers The range containing customer names.
 * @param {range} counts The range containing purchase counts for each customer.
 * @param {number} n The number of top customers to return.
 * @return {array | string} An array with the top-N customers and their purchase counts, or an error message if input data is invalid.
 * @customfunction
 */
function
TOP_N_CUSTOMERS_BY_PURCHASE_COUNT(customers,
counts, n) {
```

```
if (typeof n !== 'number' || n <= 0) return "Invalid value for N";
const data = customers.map((customer, index) => ({
customer: customer[0], count: counts[index][0] }))
 .filter(item => typeof item.customer === 'string' && typeof item.count === 'number')
 .sort((a, b) => b.count - a.count);
const result = data.slice(0, n).map(item => [item.customer, item.count]);
return result.length > 0 ? result : "No valid data!";
}
```

Steps:

1. Paste the code into a new Apps Script project.
2. Save the changes and return to Google Sheets.
3. Enter the sample data into columns A1:B8.
4. Use the function like =TOP_N_CUSTOMERS_BY_PURCHASE_COUNT(A2:A8, B2:B8, 3).

Expected Result: The function will return an array containing the top 3 customers based on purchase count.

Evaluate Sales Team Performance

D2	▼	fx =EVALUATE_SALES_PERFORMANCE(A2:A6, B2:B6, C2:C6)		
	A	B	C	D	E
1	Salesperson	Quarterly Sales	Sales Target		
2	Alice	25000	20000	Alice	Exceeded
3	Bob	19000	20000	Bob	Below
4	Carol	20000	20000	Carol	Met
5	David	30000	25000	David	Exceeded
6	Emily	15000	20000	Emily	Below

Objective: Write a function to evaluate sales team performance against quarterly targets, categorizing each member as 'Exceeded', 'Met', or 'Below' target.

Sample Data:

Salesperson	Quarterly Sales	Sales Target

Alice	25000	20000
Bob	19000	20000
Carol	20000	20000
David	30000	25000
Emily	15000	20000

Learning Outcomes:
- Learn to apply conditional logic to evaluate performance metrics.
- Practice creating insightful summaries from raw sales data.

Code Example:

```
/**
 * Evaluates sales team performance against their quarterly
targets.
 *
 * @param {range} salespeople The range containing
salesperson names.
 * @param {range} quarterlySales The range containing
quarterly sales figures.
 * @param {range} salesTargets The range containing sales
targets.
 * @return {array | string} An array listing each salesperson
with their performance category, or an error message if data
is invalid.
 * @customfunction
 */
function EVALUATE_SALES_PERFORMANCE(salespeople,
quarterlySales, salesTargets) {
const results = [];
for (let i = 0; i < salespeople.length; i++) {
const salesperson = salespeople[i][0];
const sales = quarterlySales[i][0];
const target = salesTargets[i][0];
```

```
const performance = sales > target ? 'Exceeded' : sales ===
target ? 'Met' : 'Below';
  results.push([salesperson, performance]);
  }
  return results.length > 0 ? results : "No sales data to
evaluate.";
}
```

Steps:

1. Paste the code into a new Apps Script project.
2. Save the changes and return to Google Sheets.
3. Enter the sample data into columns A1:C6.
4. Use the function like
   =EVALUATE_SALES_PERFORMANCE(A2:A6,
   B2:B6, C2:C6).

Expected Result: The function will classify each salesperson according to how well they met or exceeded their quarterly sales targets, providing clear insights into individual performances.

Calculate Employee Utilization Rate

D2	▾	_fx_ =CALCULATE_UTILIZATION_RATE(A2:A6, B2:B6, C2:C6)		
	A	B	C	D	E
1	Employee	Billable Hours	Total Hours		
2	Alice	30	40	Alice	75.00%
3	Bob	35	40	Bob	87.50%
4	Carol	40	40	Carol	100.00%
5	David	25	40	David	62.50%
6	Emily	38	40	Emily	95.00%

Objective: Write a function to calculate the utilization rate of employees based on their billable hours and total working hours.

Sample Data:

Employee	Billable Hours	Total Hours
Alice	30	40
Bob	35	40

Carol	40	40
David	25	40
Emily	38	40

Learning Outcomes:
- Learn to calculate ratios to determine efficiency.
- Practice applying mathematical formulas in a business context.

Code Example:

```
/**
 * Calculates the utilization rate for employees.
 *
 * @param {range} employees The range containing employee names.
 * @param {range} billableHours The range containing billable hours worked.
 * @param {range} totalHours The range containing total hours worked.
 * @return {array | string} An array listing each employee with their utilization rate as a percentage, or an error message if data is invalid.
 * @customfunction
 */
function CALCULATE_UTILIZATION_RATE(employees, billableHours, totalHours) {
const results = [];
for (let i = 0; i < employees.length; i++) {
const employee = employees[i][0];
const billable = billableHours[i][0];
const total = totalHours[i][0];
const utilization = (billable / total) * 100;
results.push([employee, utilization.toFixed(2) + "%"]);
}
return results.length > 0 ? results : "Invalid or empty data!";
}
```

Steps:

1. Paste the code into a new Apps Script project.
2. Save the changes and return to Google Sheets.
3. Enter the sample data into columns A1:C6.
4. Use the function like =CALCULATE_UTILIZATION_RATE(A2:A6, B2:B6, C2:C6).

Expected Result: The function will calculate and list each employee's utilization rate as a percentage, highlighting how much of their total working hours are billable.

Track Inventory Restock Needs

D2	▼	fx =TRACK_INVENTORY_RESTOCK(A2:A6, B2:B6, C2:C6)	
	A	B	C	D
1	Item	Current Stock	Minimum Required	
2	Widgets	150	200	Widgets
3	Gadgets	220	200	Thingamajig
4	Doodads	190	180	
5	Thingamajig	80	100	
6	Whatchamacallit	60	60	

Objective: Develop a function to identify inventory items that need to be restocked based on their current levels and minimum required levels.

Sample Data:

Item	Current Stock	Minimum Required
Widgets	150	200
Gadgets	220	200
Doodads	190	180
Thingamajig	80	100
Whatchamacallit	60	60

Learning Outcomes:

- Learn to filter and identify items based on stock requirements.
- Practice using conditional checks to manage inventory levels.

Code Example:

```
/**
 * Identifies inventory items that need restocking.
 *
 * @param {range} items The range containing item names.
 * @param {range} currentStock The range containing current stock levels.
 * @param {range} minimumRequired The range containing minimum required stock levels.
 * @return {array | string} An array listing items that need restocking, or an error message if all items are sufficiently stocked.
 * @customfunction
 */
function TRACK_INVENTORY_RESTOCK(items, currentStock, minimumRequired) {
const results = [];
for (let i = 0; i < items.length; i++) {
const item = items[i][0];
const stock = currentStock[i][0];
const minimum = minimumRequired[i][0];
if (stock < minimum) {
results.push([item]);
}
}
return results.length > 0 ? results : "All items are sufficiently stocked.";
}
```

Steps:

1. Paste the code into a new Apps Script project.
2. Save the changes and return to Google Sheets.
3. Enter the sample data into columns A1:C6.

4. Use the function like
   =TRACK_INVENTORY_RESTOCK(A2:A6, B2:B6, C2:C6).

Expected Result: The function will identify and list inventory items that are below the minimum required stock levels and need restocking.

Calculate Monthly Average Temperature

C2	▼	*fx* =MONTHLY_AVERAGE_TEMPERATURE(A2:A8, B2:B8)		
	A	B	C	D
1	Date	Temperature		
2	2024-01-01	15	2024-01	16.00
3	2024-01-02	17	2024-02	19.00
4	2024-02-01	20	2024-03	21.50
5	2024-02-02	18		
6	2024-02-03	19		
7	2024-03-01	22		
8	2024-03-02	21		

Objective: Write a function to calculate the average temperature for each month based on daily temperature data.

Sample Data:

Date	Temperature
2024-01-01	15
2024-01-02	17
2024-02-01	20
2024-02-02	18
2024-02-03	19
2024-03-01	22
2024-03-02	21

Learning Outcomes:
- Learn to group and average numerical data based on date components.

- Practice handling missing or incomplete data for specific periods.

Code Example:

```
/**
 * Calculates the monthly average temperature based on daily
temperature data.
 *
 * @param {range} dates The range containing the dates.
 * @param {range} temperatures The range containing
temperature readings.
 * @return {array | string} An array with the month and its
average temperature, or an error message if input data is
invalid.
 * @customfunction
 */
function MONTHLY_AVERAGE_TEMPERATURE(dates,
temperatures) {
const monthlyTemps = {};
for (let i = 0; i < dates.length; i++) {
const date = new Date(dates[i][0]);
const temp = temperatures[i][0];
if (!isNaN(date) && typeof temp === 'number') {
const monthYear = date.toISOString().slice(0, 7);
if (!monthlyTemps[monthYear]) monthlyTemps[monthYear]
= { sum: 0, count: 0 };
monthlyTemps[monthYear].sum += temp;
monthlyTemps[monthYear].count++;
}
}
const result =
Object.entries(monthlyTemps).map(([monthYear, data]) => [
monthYear, (data.sum / data.count).toFixed(2)
]);
return result.length > 0 ? result : "No valid data found!";
}
```

Steps:

1. Paste the code into a new Apps Script project.

2. Save the changes and return to Google Sheets.
3. Enter the sample data into columns A1:B8.
4. Use the function like
   =MONTHLY_AVERAGE_TEMPERATURE(A2:A8, B2:B8).

Expected Result: The function will return an array with each month and its average temperature.

5 : Dynamic Arrays and Conditional Logic

Advance your skills by integrating dynamic arrays and conditional logic into your functions. Learn to write more flexible and powerful scripts that respond to data dynamically, adjust calculations based on conditions, and handle variable data sizes efficiently.

Find the Most Common Item per Category

C2	▾	fx =MOST_COMMON_ITEM_BY_CATEGORY(A2:A9, B2:B9)		
	A	B	C	D
1	Category	Item		
2	Fruits	Apple	Fruits	Apple
3	Fruits	Banana	Vegetables	Carrot
4	Vegetables	Carrot		
5	Fruits	Apple		
6	Vegetables	Broccoli		
7	Vegetables	Carrot		
8	Fruits	Apple		
9	Vegetables	Carrot		

Objective: Write a function to find the most common item within each category.

Sample Data:

Category	Item
Fruits	Apple
Fruits	Banana
Vegetables	Carrot
Fruits	Apple
Vegetables	Broccoli
Vegetables	Carrot

Fruits	Apple
Vegetables	Carrot

Learning Outcomes:
- Learn to group items by category and count their occurrences.
- Practice conditional logic to find the most common item within a group.

Code Example:

```
/**
 * Finds the most common item within each category.
 *
 * @param {range} categories The range containing category names.
 * @param {range} items The range containing items corresponding to each category.
 * @return {array | string} An array with categories and their most common items, or an error message if input data is invalid.
 * @customfunction
 */
function MOST_COMMON_ITEM_BY_CATEGORY(categories, items) {
const itemCounts = {};
for (let i = 0; i < categories.length; i++) {
const category = categories[i][0];
const item = items[i][0];
if (typeof category === 'string' && typeof item === 'string') {
if (!itemCounts[category]) itemCounts[category] = {};
itemCounts[category][item] = (itemCounts[category][item]
|| 0) + 1;
}
}
const result = Object.entries(itemCounts).map(([category,
countMap]) => {
```

```
const mostCommonItem =
Object.entries(countMap).reduce((a, b) => (b[1] > a[1] ? b : a));
return [category, mostCommonItem[0]];
});
return result.length > 0 ? result : "Invalid or empty data!";
}
```

Steps:
1. Paste the code into a new Apps Script project.
2. Save the changes and return to Google Sheets.
3. Enter the sample data into columns A1:B9.
4. Use the function like
   =MOST_COMMON_ITEM_BY_CATEGORY(A2:A9, B2:B9).

Expected Result: The function will return an array showing each category with its most common item.

Calculate Median Score by Class

C2		_fx_ =MEDIAN_SCORE_BY_CLASS(A2:A9, B2:B9)		
	A	B	C	D
1	Class	Score		
2	A	78	A	81
3	B	85	B	90
4	A	90		
5	B	88		
6	A	70		
7	B	92		
8	A	84		
9	B	95		

Objective: Write a function to calculate the median score for each class.

Sample Data:

Class	Score
A	78
B	85
A	90

B	88
A	70
B	92
A	84
B	95

Learning Outcomes:

- Understand how to compute the median for a set of numbers.
- Learn to group and sort scores to find the median per class.

Code Example:

```
/**
 * Calculates the median score per class.
 *
 * @param {range} classes The range containing class names.
 * @param {range} scores The range containing scores for each
class.
 * @return {array | string} An array with classes and their
median scores, or an error message if input data is invalid.
 * @customfunction
 */
function MEDIAN_SCORE_BY_CLASS(classes, scores) {
  const classScores = {};
for (let i = 0; i < classes.length; i++) {
  const className = classes[i][0];
  const score = scores[i][0];
  if (typeof className === 'string' && typeof score ===
'number') {
  if (!classScores[className]) classScores[className] = [];
  classScores[className].push(score);
  }
  }
  function calculateMedian(arr) {
  arr.sort((a, b) => a - b);
```

```
const middle = Math.floor(arr.length / 2);
return arr.length % 2 === 0 ? (arr[middle - 1] + arr[middle])
/ 2 : arr[middle];
}
const result = Object.entries(classScores).map(([className,
scores]) => [className, calculateMedian(scores)]);
return result.length > 0 ? result : "Invalid or empty data!";
}
```

Steps:

1. Paste the code into a new Apps Script project.
2. Save the changes and return to Google Sheets.
3. Enter the sample data into columns A1:B9.
4. Use the function like
   =MEDIAN_SCORE_BY_CLASS(A2:A9, B2:B9).

Expected Result: The function will return an array showing each class with its median score.

Determine the Day with Maximum Sales

C2		ƒx =DAY_WITH_MAX_SALES(A2:A8, B2:B8)	
	A	B	C
1	Day	Sales	
2	Monday	150	Friday
3	Tuesday	220	300
4	Wednesday	180	
5	Thursday	240	
6	Friday	300	
7	Saturday	190	
8	Sunday	160	

Objective: Write a function to determine the day with the highest sales amount.

Sample Data:

Day	Sales
Monday	150
Tuesday	220

Wednesday	180
Thursday	240
Friday	300
Saturday	190
Sunday	160

Learning Outcomes:
- Practice identifying maximum values in a data series.
- Learn to apply conditional logic to identify the day with maximum sales.

Code Example:

```
/**
 * Determines the day with the highest sales amount.
 *
 * @param {range} days The range containing day names.
 * @param {range} sales The range containing corresponding
sales amounts.
 * @return {array | string} An array with the day and the
maximum sales amount, or an error message if input data is
invalid.
 * @customfunction
 */
function DAY_WITH_MAX_SALES(days, sales) {
let maxSales = -Infinity;
let dayWithMaxSales = "";
for (let i = 0; i < days.length; i++) {
const day = days[i][0];
const sale = sales[i][0];
if (typeof day === 'string' && typeof sale === 'number') {
if (sale > maxSales) {
maxSales = sale;
dayWithMaxSales = day;
}
}
}
```

return dayWithMaxSales ? [dayWithMaxSales, maxSales] :
"No valid data!";
}

Steps:

1. Paste the code into a new Apps Script project.
2. Save the changes and return to Google Sheets.
3. Enter the sample data into columns A1:B8.
4. Use the function like
   =DAY_WITH_MAX_SALES(A2:A8, B2:B8).

Expected Result: The function will return the day with the maximum sales amount.

Calculate Percentage of Total per Category

C2		fx =PERCENTAGE_OF_TOTAL_BY_CATEGORY(A2:A7, B2:B7)	
	A	B	C	D
1	Category	Amount		
2	Food	250	Food	11.90%
3	Travel	400	Travel	19.05%
4	Shopping	150	Shopping	7.14%
5	Rent	800	Rent	38.10%
6	Utilities	200	Utilities	9.52%
7	Savings	300	Savings	14.29%

Objective: Write a function to calculate the percentage contribution of each category to the overall total.

Sample Data:

Category	Amount
Food	250
Travel	400
Shopping	150
Rent	800
Utilities	200
Savings	300

Learning Outcomes:

- Learn to calculate and represent each category's contribution as a percentage of the total.
- Practice applying arithmetic operations to compute proportions.

Code Example:

```
/**
 * Calculates the percentage contribution of each category to
the overall total.
 *
 * @param {range} categories The range containing the
category names.
 * @param {range} amounts The range containing the
amounts corresponding to each category.
 * @return {array | string} An array with categories and their
percentages, or an error message if input data is invalid.
 * @customfunction
 */
function
PERCENTAGE_OF_TOTAL_BY_CATEGORY(categories,
amounts) {
 const totalAmount = amounts.flat().reduce((sum, amount)
=> typeof amount === 'number' ? sum + amount : sum, 0);
 if (totalAmount === 0) return "Invalid or empty data!";
 const percentages = categories.map((category, index) => {
 const amount = amounts[index][0];
 return [category[0], ((amount / totalAmount) *
100).toFixed(2) + '%'];
 });
 return percentages.length > 0 ? percentages : "No valid
data!";
}
```

Steps:
1. Paste the code into a new Apps Script project.
2. Save the changes and return to Google Sheets.
3. Enter the sample data into columns A1:B7.

4. Use the function like =PERCENTAGE_OF_TOTAL_BY_CATEGORY(A2:A7, B2:B7).

Expected Result: The function will return an array with each category's percentage contribution.

Find Items Above a Specific Quantity

C2	▾	*fx* =ITEMS_ABOVE_THRESHOLD(A2:A7, B2:B7, 100)		
	A	B	C	D
1	Item	Quantity		
2	Pencil	150	Pencil	150
3	Notebook	50	Eraser	180
4	Eraser	180	Paper	200
5	Marker	30		
6	Paper	200		
7	Stapler	60		

Objective: Write a function that returns all items whose quantities are above a specified threshold.

Sample Data:

Item	Quantity
Pencil	150
Notebook	50
Eraser	180
Marker	30
Paper	200
Stapler	60

Learning Outcomes:
- Learn to filter data based on numerical thresholds.
- Practice conditional logic to extract relevant items.

Code Example:

```
/**
```

* Returns all items whose quantities are above a specified threshold.
*
* @param {range} items The range containing item names.
* @param {range} quantities The range containing quantities for each item.
* @param {number} threshold The minimum quantity to include an item.
* @return {array | string} An array with items and their quantities, or an error message if no items are above the threshold.
* @customfunction
*/

```
function ITEMS_ABOVE_THRESHOLD(items, quantities, threshold) {
if (typeof threshold !== 'number' || threshold < 0) return "Invalid threshold";
 const result = [];
for (let i = 0; i < items.length; i++) {
 const item = items[i][0];
 const quantity = quantities[i][0];
 if (typeof item === 'string' && typeof quantity === 'number' && quantity > threshold) {
 result.push([item, quantity]);
 }
 }
 return result.length > 0 ? result : "No items above the specified threshold!";
}
```

Steps:
1. Paste the code into a new Apps Script project.
2. Save the changes and return to Google Sheets.
3. Enter the sample data into columns A1:B7.
4. Use the function like =ITEMS_ABOVE_THRESHOLD(A2:A7, B2:B7, 100).

Expected Result: The function will return an array with items and their quantities above the threshold of 100.

Identify Employees by Department

C2   ▼   _fx_ =EMPLOYEES_BY_DEPARTMENT(A2:A9, B2:B9, "IT")

	A	B	C	D
1	Employee	Department		
2	Alice	HR	David	
3	Bob	Finance	Frank	
4	Carol	Marketing		
5	David	IT		
6	Emily	HR		
7	Frank	IT		
8	George	Marketing		
9	Helen	Finance		

Objective: Write a function that identifies employees by their department.

Sample Data:

Employee	Department
Alice	HR
Bob	Finance
Carol	Marketing
David	IT
Emily	HR
Frank	IT
George	Marketing
Helen	Finance

Learning Outcomes:
- Learn to group items based on unique categories.
- Understand how to filter and list employees according to a specific department.

Code Example:

```
/**
* Lists employees by department.
*
```

* @param {range} employees The range containing employee names.
 * @param {range} departments The range containing department names.
 * @param {string} department The department name to filter by.
 * @return {array | string} An array with employee names in the specified department, or an error message if input data is invalid.
 * @customfunction
 */

```
function EMPLOYEES_BY_DEPARTMENT(employees, departments, department) {
if (typeof department !== 'string') return "Invalid department name";
 const result = [];
for (let i = 0; i < employees.length; i++) {
if (departments[i][0] === department) {
result.push([employees[i][0]]);
}
}
 return result.length > 0 ? result : "No employees found in the specified department!";
}
```

Steps:
1. Paste the code into a new Apps Script project.
2. Save the changes and return to Google Sheets.
3. Enter the sample data into columns A1:B9.
4. Use the function like =EMPLOYEES_BY_DEPARTMENT(A2:A9, B2:B9, "IT").

Expected Result: The function will return an array listing employees in the "IT" department.

Identify Outliers in Sales Data

	A	B	C	D
1	Day	Sales		
2	1	150	6	400
3	2	160		
4	3	300		
5	4	155		
6	5	145		
7	6	400		
8	7	150		

Objective: Write a function to identify outlier sales amounts using standard deviation.

Sample Data:

Day	Sales
1	150
2	160
3	300
4	155
5	145
6	400
7	150

Learning Outcomes:
- Learn to compute mean and standard deviation.
- Understand how to identify outliers using statistical methods.

Code Example:
```
/**
 * Identifies outlier sales amounts based on standard
deviation.
 *
 * @param {range} days The range containing the day
identifiers.
```

* @param {range} sales The range containing the sales amounts.
 * @return {array | string} An array listing the outlier sales amounts, or an error message if no outliers are found.
 * @customfunction
 */
```javascript
function IDENTIFY_OUTLIERS_IN_SALES(days, sales) {
  const salesData = sales.flat().filter(val => typeof val === 'number');
  if (salesData.length === 0) return "Invalid or empty data!";
  const mean = salesData.reduce((sum, val) => sum + val, 0) / salesData.length;
  const stdDev = Math.sqrt(salesData.reduce((sum, val) => sum + Math.pow(val - mean, 2), 0) / salesData.length);
  const threshold = 2 * stdDev;
  const outliers = [];
  for (let i = 0; i < salesData.length; i++) {
    if (Math.abs(salesData[i] - mean) > threshold) {
      outliers.push([days[i][0], salesData[i]]);
    }
  }
  return outliers.length > 0 ? outliers : "No outliers found!";
}
```

Steps:

1. Paste the code into a new Apps Script project.
2. Save the changes and return to Google Sheets.
3. Enter the sample data into columns A1:B8.
4. Use the function like =IDENTIFY_OUTLIERS_IN_SALES(A2:A8, B2:B8).

Expected Result: The function will return an array listing days and their outlier sales amounts.

Calculate Total Revenue per Salesperson

C2 ▾ fx =TOTAL_REVENUE_PER_SALESPERSON(A2:A8, B2:B8)

	A	B	C	D
1	Salesperson	Sale Amount		
2	Alice	1200	Alice	4100.00
3	Bob	900	Bob	1700.00
4	Alice	1500	Carol	3300.00
5	Carol	2000		
6	Bob	800		
7	Carol	1300		
8	Alice	1400		

Objective: Write a function to calculate the total revenue generated by each salesperson.

Sample Data:

Salesperson	Sale Amount
Alice	1200
Bob	900
Alice	1500
Carol	2000
Bob	800
Carol	1300
Alice	1400

Learning Outcomes:
- Practice grouping data by salesperson.
- Understand how to aggregate sales amounts to calculate total revenue.

Code Example:
```
/**
* Calculates the total revenue generated by each salesperson.
*
* @param {range} salespeople The range containing
salesperson names.
```

```
 * @param {range} amounts The range containing sales
amounts.
 * @return {array | string} An array with salesperson names
and their total revenue, or an error message if no data is
available.
 * @customfunction
 */
function
TOTAL_REVENUE_PER_SALESPERSON(salespeople,
amounts) {
 const revenue = {};
for (let i = 0; i < salespeople.length; i++) {
 const salesperson = salespeople[i][0];
 const amount = amounts[i][0];
 if (typeof salesperson === 'string' && typeof amount ===
'number') {
 revenue[salesperson] = (revenue[salesperson] || 0) +
amount;
 }
 }
 const result = Object.entries(revenue).map(([salesperson,
total]) => [salesperson, total.toFixed(2)]);
 return result.length > 0 ? result : "No valid data!";
}
```

Steps:
1. Paste the code into a new Apps Script project.
2. Save the changes and return to Google Sheets.
3. Enter the sample data into columns A1:B8.
4. Use the function like
    =TOTAL_REVENUE_PER_SALESPERSON(A2:A8,
    B2:B8).

Expected Result: The function will return an array listing
each salesperson and their total revenue.

Calculate Average Project Duration by Team

C2	▾	fx =AVERAGE_PROJECT_DURATION_BY_TEAM(A2:A9, B2:B9)		
	A	B	C	D
1	Team	Project Duration (days)		
2	Red	30	Red	28.33
3	Blue	45	Blue	50.00
4	Green	60	Green	50.00
5	Red	20		
6	Blue	50		
7	Green	40		
8	Red	35		
9	Blue	55		

Objective: Write a function to calculate the average project duration for each team.

Sample Data:

Team	Project Duration (days)
Red	30
Blue	45
Green	60
Red	20
Blue	50
Green	40
Red	35
Blue	55

Learning Outcomes:
- Practice calculating averages for grouped data.
- Learn to work with numerical data and aggregate by team.

Code Example:
```
/**
* Calculates the average project duration for each team.
```

```
 *
 * @param {range} teams The range containing team names.
 * @param {range} durations The range containing project
durations in days.
 * @return {array | string} An array with team names and their
average project duration, or an error message if no data is
available.
 * @customfunction
 */
function
AVERAGE_PROJECT_DURATION_BY_TEAM(teams,
durations) {
 const teamDurations = {};
for (let i = 0; i < teams.length; i++) {
 const team = teams[i][0];
 const duration = durations[i][0];
 if (typeof team === 'string' && typeof duration ===
'number') {
 if (!teamDurations[team]) teamDurations[team] = { total: 0,
count: 0 };
 teamDurations[team].total += duration;
 teamDurations[team].count++;
 }
 }
 const result = Object.entries(teamDurations).map((([team,
data]) => [
 team, (data.total / data.count).toFixed(2)
 ]);
 return result.length > 0 ? result : "No valid data!";
}
```

Steps:

1. Paste the code into a new Apps Script project.
2. Save the changes and return to Google Sheets.
3. Enter the sample data into columns A1:B9.
4. Use the function like
   =AVERAGE_PROJECT_DURATION_BY_TEAM(A2:
   A9, B2:B9).

Expected Result: The function will return an array listing each team and their average project duration.

Calculate Grade Distribution

C2	▾	f_x =GRADE_DISTRIBUTION(A2:A9, B2:B9)		
	A	B	C	D
1	Student	Score		
2	Alice	85	A (85-100)	3
3	Bob	70	B (70-84)	3
4	Carol	92	C (55-69)	2
5	David	76	F (0-54)	0
6	Emily	65		
7	Frank	55		
8	George	88		
9	Helen	78		

Objective: Write a function to calculate the number of students in each grade range.

Sample Data:

Student	Score
Alice	85
Bob	70
Carol	92
David	76
Emily	65
Frank	55
George	88
Helen	78

Learning Outcomes:
- Learn to categorize data based on predefined ranges.
- Understand how to count items within specific grade ranges.

Code Example:

```
/**
 * Calculates the distribution of students across grade ranges.
 *
 * @param {range} students The range containing student
 * names.
 * @param {range} scores The range containing scores.
 * @return {array | string} An array with grade ranges and
 * counts, or an error message if input data is invalid.
 * @customfunction
 */
function GRADE_DISTRIBUTION(students, scores) {
 const distribution = { "A (85-100)": 0, "B (70-84)": 0, "C (55-
69)": 0, "F (0-54)": 0 };
for (let i = 0; i < scores.length; i++) {
 const score = scores[i][0];
 if (typeof score === 'number') {
 if (score >= 85 && score <= 100) distribution["A (85-100)"]++;
 else if (score >= 70 && score <= 84) distribution["B (70-
84)"]++;
 else if (score >= 55 && score <= 69) distribution["C (55-
69)"]++;
 else distribution["F (0-54)"]++;
 }
 }
 const result = Object.entries(distribution).map((([range,
count]) => [range, count]);
 return result.length > 0 ? result : "Invalid or empty data!";
}
```

Steps:

1. Paste the code into a new Apps Script project.
2. Save the changes and return to Google Sheets.
3. Enter the sample data into columns A1:B9.
4. Use the function like
   =GRADE_DISTRIBUTION(A2:A9, B2:B9).

Expected Result: The function will return an array showing the count of students in each grade range.

Calculate Monthly Sales Growth

C2   ▼   *fx* =MONTHLY_SALES_GROWTH(A2:A7, B2:B7)

	A	B	C	D
1	Month	Sales		
2	January	1000	Month	Growth %
3	February	1100	February	10.00%
4	March	1200	March	9.09%
5	April	1250	April	4.17%
6	May	1150	May	-8.00%
7	June	1400	June	21.74%
8				

Objective: Write a function to calculate the month-over-month sales growth.

Sample Data:

Month	Sales
January	1000
February	1100
March	1200
April	1250
May	1150
June	1400

Learning Outcomes:
- Understand how to calculate growth percentages between consecutive months.
- Learn to manipulate numerical data and apply conditional logic.

Code Example:

```
/**
* Calculates the month-over-month sales growth.
*
* @param {range} months The range containing the month
names.
* @param {range} sales The range containing sales data.
```

* @return {array | string} An array with months and their growth percentages, or an error message if input data is invalid.
* @customfunction
*/

```javascript
function MONTHLY_SALES_GROWTH(months, sales) {
const growth = [["Month", "Growth %"]];
for (let i = 1; i < months.length; i++) {
const month = months[i][0];
const prevSales = sales[i - 1][0];
const currSales = sales[i][0];
if (typeof prevSales !== 'number' || typeof currSales !==
'number') {
return "Invalid or empty data!";
}
const growthPercentage = ((currSales - prevSales) /
prevSales) * 100;
growth.push([month, growthPercentage.toFixed(2) + "%"]);
}
return growth.length > 1 ? growth : "Not enough data!";
}
```

Steps:

1. Paste the code into a new Apps Script project.
2. Save the changes and return to Google Sheets.
3. Enter the sample data into columns A1:B7.
4. Use the function like
   =MONTHLY_SALES_GROWTH(A2:A7, B2:B7).

Expected Result: The function will return an array showing the month-over-month sales growth percentages.

6 : Common Business Solutions

Output of cell data values using various calculations to create useful insights and data outputs for the values within the columns.

Analyze Monthly Sales Growth

C2		fx =ANALYZE_MONTHLY_SALES_GROWTH(A2:A6, B2:B6)		
	A	B	C	D
1	Month	Sales		
2	January	10000	February	5.00%
3	February	10500	March	4.76%
4	March	11000	April	4.55%
5	April	11500	May	4.35%
6	May	12000		

Objective: Create a function to analyze monthly sales growth by comparing sales figures month-over-month and identifying the percentage change.

Sample Data:

Month	Sales
January	10000
February	10500
March	11000
April	11500
May	12000

Learning Outcomes:
- Practice calculating percentage changes between sequential data points.
- Learn to provide insights into sales trends over time.

Code Example:

```
/**
 * Analyzes monthly sales growth, calculating the percentage
change from the previous month.
 *
 * @param {range} months The range containing month
names.
 * @param {range} sales The range containing sales figures for
each month.
 * @return {array | string} An array listing each month with
the percentage change in sales from the previous month, or
an error message if data is invalid.
 * @customfunction
 */
function ANALYZE_MONTHLY_SALES_GROWTH(months,
sales) {
 const results = [];
for (let i = 1; i < months.length; i++) {
 const month = months[i][0];
 const previousSales = sales[i - 1][0];
 const currentSales = sales[i][0];
 const growthRate = ((currentSales - previousSales) /
previousSales) * 100;
 results.push([month, growthRate.toFixed(2) + "%"]);
 }
 return results.length > 0 ? results : "Insufficient data for
growth analysis.";
}
```

Steps:

1. Paste the code into a new Apps Script project.
2. Save the changes and return to Google Sheets.
3. Enter the sample data into columns A1:B6.
4. Use the function like
    =ANALYZE_MONTHLY_SALES_GROWTH(A2:A6,
    B2:B6).

Expected Result: The function will calculate and list the percentage change in sales for each month compared to the previous month, providing a clear view of sales growth trends.

Calculate Product Profitability

D2		fx =CALCULATE_PRODUCT_PROFITABILITY(A2:A6, B2:B6, C2:C6)			
	A	B	C	D	E
1	Product	Sales Revenue	Cost of Goods Sold		
2	Widget	12000	8000	Widget	4000
3	Gadget	20000	15000	Gadget	5000
4	Gizmo	15000	7000	Gizmo	8000
5	Thingy	8000	3000	Thingy	5000
6	Doodad	5000	4500	Doodad	500

Objective: Write a function to calculate the profitability of products based on their sales and cost data.
Sample Data:

Product	Sales Revenue	Cost of Goods Sold
Widget	12000	8000
Gadget	20000	15000
Gizmo	15000	7000
Thingy	8000	3000
Doodad	5000	4500

Learning Outcomes:
- Learn to calculate net profitability (sales revenue minus cost).
- Practice basic arithmetic operations within a business context.

Code Example:
```
/**
* Calculates the profitability of products.
*
```

* @param {range} products The range containing product names.
 * @param {range} salesRevenue The range containing sales revenue figures.
 * @param {range} costs The range containing cost of goods sold.
 * @return {array | string} An array listing each product with its profitability, or an error message if data is invalid.
 * @customfunction
 */

```
function
CALCULATE_PRODUCT_PROFITABILITY(products,
salesRevenue, costs) {
 const results = [];
 for (let i = 0; i < products.length; i++) {
 const product = products[i][0];
 const revenue = salesRevenue[i][0];
 const cost = costs[i][0];
 const profitability = revenue - cost;
 results.push([product, profitability]);
 }
 return results.length > 0 ? results : "Invalid or empty data!";
}
```

Steps:
1. Paste the code into a new Apps Script project.
2. Save the changes and return to Google Sheets.
3. Enter the sample data into columns A1:C6.
4. Use the function like =CALCULATE_PRODUCT_PROFITABILITY(A2:A6, B2:B6, C2:C6).

Expected Result: The function will calculate and list the profitability for each product, helping businesses understand which products are generating profit and which are not.

Assess Employee On-Time Arrival

Objective: Develop a function to identify employees who consistently arrive on time over a week.

Sample Data:

Employee	Day 1	Day 2	Day 3	Day 4	Day 5
Alice	On Time	Late	On Time	On Time	On Time
Bob	On Time	On Time	On Time	On Time	On Time
Carol	Late	On Time	Late	On Time	On Time
David	On Time	On Time	Late	On Time	Late
Emily	On Time	On Time	On Time	On Time	On Time

Learning Outcomes:
- Practice using conditional checks to evaluate attendance records.
- Learn to aggregate and summarize data to determine reliability.

Code Example:
```
/**
* Identifies employees who are consistently on time.
*
* @param {range} employees The range containing employee
names.
* @param {range} days The range containing attendance
status for multiple days.
* @return {array | string} An array listing employees who are
consistently on time, or an error message if data is invalid.
* @customfunction
*/
```

```javascript
function ASSESS_ON_TIME_ARRIVAL(employees, days) {
const results = [];
for (let i = 0; i < employees.length; i++) {
const employee = employees[i][0];
const daysArray = days[i];
const allOnTime = daysArray.every(status => status === "On
Time");
if (allOnTime) {
results.push([employee]);
}
}
return results.length > 0 ? results : "No consistently on-time
employees.";
}
```

Steps:

1. Paste the code into a new Apps Script project.
2. Save the changes and return to Google Sheets.
3. Enter the sample data into columns A1:F6.
4. Use the function like
   =ASSESS_ON_TIME_ARRIVAL(A2:A6, B2:F6).

Expected Result: The function will identify employees who arrived on time every day of the week, highlighting their punctuality.

Monitor Contract Expiration Dates

C2	▼	ƒx	=MONITOR_CONTRACT_EXPIRATIONS(A2:A6, B2:B6)	

	A	B	C	D
1	Contract ID	Expiration Date		
2	3	2024-05-15		4	2024-06-15
3	4	2024-06-15		
4	5	2024-05-10		

Objective: Create a function to monitor and alert about contracts that are due to expire within the next month.
Sample Data:

Contract ID	Expiration Date
3	2024-05-15
4	2024-06-15
5	2024-05-10

Learning Outcomes:
- Practice working with date comparisons to handle timely reminders.
- Learn to create functions that can aid in proactive management tasks.

Code Example:
```
/**
 * Monitors and alerts about contracts due to expire within
the next month.
 *
 * @param {range} contractIDs The range containing contract
IDs.
 * @param {range} expirationDates The range containing
expiration dates.
 * @return {array | string} An array listing contracts expiring
within the next month, or an error message if no such
contracts are found.
 * @customfunction
 */
function
MONITOR_CONTRACT_EXPIRATIONS(contractIDs,
expirationDates) {
const today = new Date();
const nextMonth = new Date(today.getFullYear(),
today.getMonth() + 1, today.getDate());
const results = [];
for (let i = 0; i < contractIDs.length; i++) {
const contractID = contractIDs[i][0];
const expirationDate = new Date(expirationDates[i][0]);
```

```
  if (expirationDate >= today && expirationDate <=
nextMonth) {
  results.push([contractID,
expirationDate.toISOString().split('T')[0]]);
  }
}
  return results.length > 0 ? results : "No contracts expiring
within the next month.";
}
```

Steps:

1. Paste the code into a new Apps Script project.
2. Save the changes and return to Google Sheets.
3. Enter the sample data into columns A1:B6.
4. Use the function like
   =MONITOR_CONTRACT_EXPIRATIONS(A2:A6,
   B2:B6).

Expected Result: The function will list all contracts that are due to expire within the next month, providing timely reminders to review and manage these contracts appropriately. This setup helps in proactive contract management, ensuring that no critical deadlines are missed.

Find Products Below Stock Threshold

C2		f_x =PRODUCTS_BELOW_STOCK_THRESHOLD(A2:A7, B2:B7, 10)		
	A	B	C	D
1	Product	Stock		
2	Pen	15	Eraser	5
3	Notebook	10	Stapler	8
4	Eraser	5		
5	Marker	20		
6	Paper	12		
7	Stapler	8		

Objective: Write a function that identifies products whose stock is below a specified threshold.

Sample Data:

Product	Stock

Pen	15
Notebook	10
Eraser	5
Marker	20
Paper	12
Stapler	8

Learning Outcomes:
- Learn to filter and identify products whose stock is below a specific number.
- Understand how to work with conditional logic for numerical data.

Code Example:

```
/**
 * Identifies products whose stock is below a specified
threshold.
 *
 * @param {range} products The range containing product
names.
 * @param {range} stocks The range containing stock levels.
 * @param {number} threshold The stock level below which to
include a product.
 * @return {array | string} An array with products and their
stock levels, or an error message if no data is found.
 * @customfunction
 */
function
PRODUCTS_BELOW_STOCK_THRESHOLD(products,
stocks, threshold) {
 if (typeof threshold !== 'number' || threshold < 0) return
"Invalid threshold value";
 const result = [];
 for (let i = 0; i < products.length; i++) {
 const product = products[i][0];
 const stock = stocks[i][0];
```

```
if (typeof product === 'string' && typeof stock === 'number'
&& stock < threshold) {
result.push([product, stock]);
}
}
return result.length > 0 ? result : "No products below the
specified stock threshold!";
}
```

Steps:
1. Paste the code into a new Apps Script project.
2. Save the changes and return to Google Sheets.
3. Enter the sample data into columns A1:B7.
4. Use the function like
   =PRODUCTS_BELOW_STOCK_THRESHOLD(A2:A7
   , B2:B7, 10).

Expected Result: The function will return an array listing the products below the specified stock threshold.

Calculate Profit Margin per Product

D2	▾	*fx* =PROFIT_MARGIN_PER_PRODUCT(A2:A7, B2:B7, C2:C7)		
	A	B	C	D	E
1	Product	Cost	Selling Price		
2	Laptop	800	1000	Laptop	20.00%
3	Smartphone	300	450	Smartphone	33.33%
4	Tablet	200	350	Tablet	42.86%
5	Headphones	50	120	Headphones	58.33%
6	Keyboard	40	60	Keyboard	33.33%
7	Monitor	150	220	Monitor	31.82%

Objective: Write a function to calculate the profit margin for each product given the cost and selling price.

Sample Data:

Product	Cost	Selling Price
Laptop	800	1000
Smartphone	300	450
Tablet	200	350

Headphones	50	120
Keyboard	40	60
Monitor	150	220

Learning Outcomes:
- Learn to apply arithmetic operations to calculate profit margins.
- Understand how to work with cost and selling price to calculate percentages.

Code Example:

```
/**
 * Calculates the profit margin for each product.
 *
 * @param {range} products The range containing product
names.
 * @param {range} costs The range containing the cost prices.
 * @param {range} sellingPrices The range containing the
selling prices.
 * @return {array | string} An array with products and their
profit margins, or an error message if input data is invalid.
 * @customfunction
 */
function PROFIT_MARGIN_PER_PRODUCT(products, costs,
sellingPrices) {
const result = [];
for (let i = 0; i < products.length; i++) {
const product = products[i][0];
const cost = costs[i][0];
const sellingPrice = sellingPrices[i][0];
if (typeof product === 'string' && typeof cost === 'number'
&& typeof sellingPrice === 'number') {
const margin = ((sellingPrice - cost) / sellingPrice) * 100;
result.push([product, margin.toFixed(2) + '%']);
}
}
return result.length > 0 ? result : "Invalid or empty data!";
```

}
Steps:
1. Paste the code into a new Apps Script project.
2. Save the changes and return to Google Sheets.
3. Enter the sample data into columns A1:C7.
4. Use the function like
   =PROFIT_MARGIN_PER_PRODUCT(A2:A7, B2:B7, C2:C7).

Expected Result: The function will return an array listing each product with its profit margin.

Calculate Employee Salaries After Bonus

D2	▾	fx =FINAL_SALARIES_AFTER_BONUS(A2:A7, B2:B7, C2:C7)		
	A	B	C	D	E
1	Employee	Base Salary	Bonus (%)		
2	Alice	50000	10	Alice	55000.00
3	Bob	45000	15	Bob	51750.00
4	Carol	60000	5	Carol	63000.00
5	David	55000	12	David	61600.00
6	Emily	48000	8	Emily	51840.00
7	Frank	53000	10	Frank	58300.00

Objective: Write a function to calculate the final salaries after adding a bonus for each employee.

Sample Data:

Employee	Base Salary	Bonus (%)
Alice	50000	10
Bob	45000	15
Carol	60000	5
David	55000	12
Emily	48000	8
Frank	53000	10

Learning Outcomes:
- Learn to apply bonus percentages to base salaries.

- Practice arithmetic operations to compute final salaries.

Code Example:

```
/**
* Calculates the final salaries of employees after adding
bonuses.
*
* @param {range} employees The range containing employee
names.
* @param {range} salaries The range containing base salaries.
* @param {range} bonuses The range containing bonus
percentages.
* @return {array | string} An array with employees and their
final salaries, or an error message if input data is invalid.
* @customfunction
*/
function FINAL_SALARIES_AFTER_BONUS(employees,
salaries, bonuses) {
const result = [];
for (let i = 0; i < employees.length; i++) {
const employee = employees[i][0];
const salary = salaries[i][0];
const bonus = bonuses[i][0];
if (typeof employee === 'string' && typeof salary ===
'number' && typeof bonus === 'number') {
const finalSalary = salary + (salary * (bonus / 100));
result.push([employee, finalSalary.toFixed(2)]);
}
}
return result.length > 0 ? result : "Invalid or empty data!";
}
```

Steps:
1. Paste the code into a new Apps Script project.
2. Save the changes and return to Google Sheets.
3. Enter the sample data into columns A1:C7.

4. Use the function like
    =FINAL_SALARIES_AFTER_BONUS(A2:A7, B2:B7,
    C2:C7).

Expected Result: The function will return an array listing each employee with their final salary after applying the bonus.

Find Top-N Sales Regions

C2	▼	*ƒx* =TOP_N_SALES_REGIONS(A2:A9, B2:B9, 3)		
	A	B	C	D
1	Region	Sales		
2	East	15000	North	34000.00
3	West	12000	East	28000.00
4	North	18000	West	23000.00
5	South	14000		
6	Central	17000		
7	East	13000		
8	North	16000		
9	West	11000		

Objective: Write a function that identifies the top-N regions with the highest total sales.
Sample Data:

Region	Sales
East	15000
West	12000
North	18000
South	14000
Central	17000
East	13000
North	16000
West	11000

Learning Outcomes:
- Learn to aggregate sales data by region.
- Practice filtering the top-N regions based on total sales.

Code Example:

```
/**
 * Identifies the top-N sales regions based on total sales.
 *
 * @param {range} regions The range containing region names.
 * @param {range} sales The range containing the sales data.
 * @param {number} n The number of top regions to return.
 * @return {array | string} An array with regions and their total sales, or an error message if input data is invalid.
 * @customfunction
 */
function TOP_N_SALES_REGIONS(regions, sales, n) {
if (typeof n !== 'number' || n <= 0) return "Invalid value for N";
const regionSales = {};
for (let i = 0; i < regions.length; i++) {
const region = regions[i][0];
const sale = sales[i][0];
if (typeof region === 'string' && typeof sale === 'number') {
regionSales[region] = (regionSales[region] || 0) + sale;
}
}
const result = Object.entries(regionSales).sort((a, b) => b[1] -
a[1]).slice(0, n).map(([region, total]) => [region,
total.toFixed(2)]);
return result.length > 0 ? result : "No valid data!";
}
```

Steps:
1. Paste the code into a new Apps Script project.
2. Save the changes and return to Google Sheets.
3. Enter the sample data into columns A1:B9.

4. Use the function like
   =TOP_N_SALES_REGIONS(A2:A9, B2:B9, 3).

Expected Result: The function will return an array listing the top 3 regions with the highest total sales.

Calculate Average Age per Department

D2		▾	fx =AVERAGE_AGE_BY_DEPARTMENT(A2:A8, C2:C8)	

	A	B	C	D	E
1	Department	Employee	Age		
2	HR	Alice	28	HR	30.00
3	IT	Bob	35	IT	40.00
4	Marketing	Carol	30	Marketing	29.50
5	IT	David	40		
6	HR	Emily	32		
7	Marketing	Frank	29		
8	IT	George	45		

Objective: Write a function to calculate the average age of employees in each department.

Sample Data:

Department	Employee	Age
HR	Alice	28
IT	Bob	35
Marketing	Carol	30
IT	David	40
HR	Emily	32
Marketing	Frank	29
IT	George	45

Learning Outcomes:
- Practice grouping data by department and calculating averages.
- Learn how to manipulate numerical data to compute average age.

Code Example:

```
/**
 * Calculates the average age of employees in each
department.
 *
 * @param {range} departments The range containing
department names.
 * @param {range} ages The range containing the ages of
employees.
 * @return {array | string} An array with department names
and their average age, or an error message if input data is
invalid.
 * @customfunction
 */
function AVERAGE_AGE_BY_DEPARTMENT(departments,
ages) {
const departmentAges = {};
for (let i = 0; i < departments.length; i++) {
const department = departments[i][0];
const age = ages[i][0];
if (typeof department === 'string' && typeof age ===
'number') {
if (!departmentAges[department])
departmentAges[department] = { total: 0, count: 0 };
departmentAges[department].total += age;
departmentAges[department].count++;
}
}
const result =
Object.entries(departmentAges).map((([department, data]) =>
[
department, (data.total / data.count).toFixed(2)
]);
return result.length > 0 ? result : "No valid data!";
}
```
Steps:
1. Paste the code into a new Apps Script project.
2. Save the changes and return to Google Sheets.

3. Enter the sample data into columns A1:C8.
4. Use the function like =AVERAGE_AGE_BY_DEPARTMENT(A2:A8, C2:C8).

Expected Result: The function will return an array listing each department and its average age.

Count Projects per Team

C2	▾	fx =COUNT_PROJECTS_PER_TEAM(A2:A8, B2:B8)		
	A	B	C	D
1	Team	Project		
2	Red	Project Alpha	Red	3
3	Blue	Project Beta	Blue	2
4	Green	Project Gamma	Green	2
5	Red	Project Delta		
6	Blue	Project Epsilon		
7	Green	Project Zeta		
8	Red	Project Eta		

Objective: Write a function that counts the number of projects assigned to each team.

Sample Data:

Team	Project
Red	Project Alpha
Blue	Project Beta
Green	Project Gamma
Red	Project Delta
Blue	Project Epsilon
Green	Project Zeta
Red	Project Eta

Learning Outcomes:
- Learn to group and count items by team.
- Practice filtering and grouping data to count project assignments.

Code Example:

```
/**
 * Counts the number of projects assigned to each team.
 *
 * @param {range} teams The range containing team names.
 * @param {range} projects The range containing project
names.
 * @return {array|string} An array with teams and their
project counts, or an error message if input data is invalid.
 * @customfunction
 */
function COUNT_PROJECTS_PER_TEAM(teams, projects) {
const projectCounts = {};
for (let i = 0; i < teams.length; i++) {
const team = teams[i][0];
if (typeof team === 'string') {
projectCounts[team] = (projectCounts[team] || 0) + 1;
}
}
const result = Object.entries(projectCounts).map((([team,
count]) => [team, count]);
return result.length > 0 ? result : "No valid data!";
}
```

Steps:
1. Paste the code into a new Apps Script project.
2. Save the changes and return to Google Sheets.
3. Enter the sample data into columns A1:B8.
4. Use the function like
   =COUNT_PROJECTS_PER_TEAM(A2:A8, B2:B8).

Expected Result: The function will return an array listing each team and the count of projects assigned.

Identify Customers with Multiple Purchases

	A	B	C	D
1	Customer	Purchase		
2	Alice	Order 1	Alice	3
3	Bob	Order 2	Bob	2
4	Carol	Order 3	Carol	2
5	Alice	Order 4		
6	Bob	Order 5		
7	Alice	Order 6		
8	Carol	Order 7		
9	David	Order 8		

Objective: Write a function to identify customers who have made multiple purchases.

Sample Data:

Customer	Purchase
Alice	Order 1
Bob	Order 2
Carol	Order 3
Alice	Order 4
Bob	Order 5
Alice	Order 6
Carol	Order 7
David	Order 8

Learning Outcomes:
- Learn to identify customers with multiple purchases.
- Practice grouping and filtering data to detect repeated items.

Code Example:

```
/**
 * Identifies customers who have made multiple purchases.
 *
```

```
 * @param {range} customers The range containing customer
names.
 * @param {range} purchases The range containing purchase
information.
 * @return {array | string} An array with customer names and
their purchase counts, or an error message if no customers are
found.
 * @customfunction
 */
function MULTIPLE_PURCHASE_CUSTOMERS(customers,
purchases) {
const customerCounts = {};
const result = [];
for (let i = 0; i < customers.length; i++) {
const customer = customers[i][0];
if (typeof customer === 'string') {
customerCounts[customer] = (customerCounts[customer] ||
0) + 1;
}
}
Object.entries(customerCounts).forEach(([customer, count])
=> {
if (count > 1) {
result.push([customer, count]);
}
});
return result.length > 0 ? result : "No customers with
multiple purchases found!";
}
```

Steps:

1. Paste the code into a new Apps Script project.
2. Save the changes and return to Google Sheets.
3. Enter the sample data into columns A1:B9.
4. Use the function like
   =MULTIPLE_PURCHASE_CUSTOMERS(A2:A9,
   B2:B9).

Expected Result: The function will return an array showing customers who have made more than one purchase, along with their purchase counts.

Calculate Total Time Spent on Tasks

C2	▼	fx =TOTAL_TIME_SPENT(A2:A8, B2:B8)	
	A	B	C
1	Task	Hours	
2	Research	5	31
3	Development	10	
4	Testing	4	
5	Documentation	3	
6	Meeting	2	
7	Review	1	
8	Debugging	6	

Objective: Write a function to calculate the total time spent on tasks, assuming each task is recorded in hours.

Sample Data:

Task	Hours
Research	5
Development	10
Testing	4
Documentation	3
Meeting	2
Review	1
Debugging	6

Learning Outcomes:
- Learn to aggregate time spent on tasks.
- Practice using arithmetic operations to calculate total time.

Code Example:

```
/**
 * Calculates the total time spent on tasks.
 *
 * @param {range} tasks The range containing task names.
 * @param {range} hours The range containing hours spent on
each task.
 * @return {number | string} The total time spent on tasks, or
an error message if input data is invalid.
 * @customfunction
 */
function TOTAL_TIME_SPENT(tasks, hours) {
  const totalHours = hours.flat().reduce((sum, value) => typeof
value === 'number' ? sum + value : sum, 0);
  return totalHours > 0 ? totalHours : "Invalid or empty data!";
}
```

Steps:
1. Paste the code into a new Apps Script project.
2. Save the changes and return to Google Sheets.
3. Enter the sample data into columns A1:B8.
4. Use the function like =TOTAL_TIME_SPENT(A2:A8, B2:B8).

Expected Result: The function will return the total number of hours spent on all tasks.

Find Items Within Price Range

C2	▾	fx =ITEMS_WITHIN_PRICE_RANGE(A2:A8, B2:B8, 100, 500)		
	A	B	C	D
1	Item	Price		
2	Laptop	900	Smartphone	450
3	Smartphone	450	Tablet	300
4	Tablet	300	Headphones	120
5	Headphones	120	Monitor	220
6	Monitor	220		
7	Keyboard	60		
8	Mouse	30		

Objective: Write a function to find items whose prices fall within a given range.

Sample Data:

Item	Price
Laptop	900
Smartphone	450
Tablet	300
Headphones	120
Monitor	220
Keyboard	60
Mouse	30

Learning Outcomes:
- Practice filtering data based on a numerical range.
- Understand conditional logic to identify items within the specified range.

Code Example:

```
/**
 * Finds items within a specified price range.
 *
 * @param {range} items The range containing item names.
 * @param {range} prices The range containing prices of items.
 * @param {number} minPrice The minimum price to include an item.
 * @param {number} maxPrice The maximum price to include an item.
 * @return {array | string} An array listing items and their prices within the specified range, or an error message if no items are found.
 * @customfunction
 */
function ITEMS_WITHIN_PRICE_RANGE(items, prices, minPrice, maxPrice) {
  if (typeof minPrice !== 'number' || minPrice < 0 || typeof maxPrice !== 'number' || maxPrice < minPrice) {
    return "Invalid price range!";
```

```
}
const result = [];
for (let i = 0; i < items.length; i++) {
const item = items[i][0];
const price = prices[i][0];
if (typeof item === 'string' && typeof price === 'number' &&
price >= minPrice && price <= maxPrice) {
result.push([item, price]);
}
}
return result.length > 0 ? result : "No items within the
specified price range!";
}
```

Steps:

1. Paste the code into a new Apps Script project.
2. Save the changes and return to Google Sheets.
3. Enter the sample data into columns A1:B8.
4. Use the function like
   =ITEMS_WITHIN_PRICE_RANGE(A2:A8, B2:B8, 100, 500).

Expected Result: The function will return an array of items and their prices within the specified range.

List Employees with Specific Skill

C2	▼	_fx_ =EMPLOYEES_WITH_SKILL(A2:A8, B2:B8, "Python")		
	A	B	C	D
1	Employee	Skills		
2	Alice	Java, Python	Alice	
3	Bob	Python, C++	Bob	
4	Carol	HTML, CSS	Emily	
5	David	Java, JavaScript	Frank	
6	Emily	Python, HTML		
7	Frank	SQL, Python		
8	George	Java, C++		

Objective: Write a function to list employees who possess a specific skill.

Sample Data:

Employee	Skills
Alice	Java, Python
Bob	Python, C++
Carol	HTML, CSS
David	Java, JavaScript
Emily	Python, HTML
Frank	SQL, Python
George	Java, C++

Learning Outcomes:
- Learn to identify and list employees based on specific skills.
- Understand string matching and filtering using JavaScript methods.

Code Example:

```
/**
 * Lists employees who possess a specific skill.
 *
 * @param {range} employees The range containing employee
names.
 * @param {range} skills The range containing skills for each
employee.
 * @param {string} skill The specific skill to search for.
 * @return {array|string} An array listing employees with the
specified skill, or an error message if no matching employees
are found.
 * @customfunction
 */
function EMPLOYEES_WITH_SKILL(employees, skills, skill)
{
if (typeof skill !== 'string' || skill.trim() === '') return
"Invalid skill input!";
 const result = [];
for (let i = 0; i < employees.length; i++) {
```

```
  if (skills[i][0] &&
skills[i][0].toLowerCase().includes(skill.toLowerCase())) {
  result.push([employees[i][0]]);
  }
}
return result.length > 0 ? result : "No employees with the
specified skill!";
}
```

Steps:

1. Paste the code into a new Apps Script project.
2. Save the changes and return to Google Sheets.
3. Enter the sample data into columns A1:B8.
4. Use the function like
    =EMPLOYEES_WITH_SKILL(A2:A8, B2:B8,
    "Python").

Expected Result: The function will return an array listing employees who possess the "Python" skill.

7 : Apps Script custom Sheet Examples

In this section the examples presented will demonstrate how to get multiple rows and columns of data and also output multiple rows and columns of response data.

Find the Most Frequent Customer Visits

C2		▾	f_x =TOP_N_FREQUENT_CUSTOMERS(A2:A9, B2:B9, 3)		
	A	B	C	D
1	Customer	Visit Count		
2	Alice	10	David	20
3	Bob	8	George	18
4	Carol	15	Carol	15
5	David	20		
6	Emily	12		
7	Frank	5		
8	George	18		
9	Helen	9		

Objective: Write a function to find the customers who have visited the most number of times.
Sample Data:

Customer	Visit Count
Alice	10
Bob	8
Carol	15
David	20
Emily	12
Frank	5
George	18
Helen	9

Learning Outcomes:
- Learn to identify and filter customers based on their visit count.
- Understand how to find the top-N frequent customers.

Code Example:

```
/**
 * Finds the customers with the most frequent visits.
 *
 * @param {range} customers The range containing customer
names.
 * @param {range} visits The range containing visit counts.
 * @param {number} n The number of top frequent customers
to return.
 * @return {array | string} An array listing the top-N frequent
customers and their visit counts, or an error message if input
data is invalid.
 * @customfunction
 */
function TOP_N_FREQUENT_CUSTOMERS(customers,
visits, n) {
if (typeof n !== 'number' || n <= 0) return "Invalid value for
N";
const data = customers.map((customer, index) => ({
customer: customer[0], count: visits[index][0] }))
.filter(item => typeof item.customer === 'string' && typeof
item.count === 'number')
.sort((a, b) => b.count - a.count);
const result = data.slice(0, n).map(item => [item.customer,
item.count]);
return result.length > 0 ? result : "No valid data!";
}
```

Steps:
1. Paste this code into a new Apps Script project.
2. Save the changes and return to Google Sheets.
3. Enter the sample data into columns A1:B9.

4. Use the function like
   =TOP_N_FREQUENT_CUSTOMERS(A2:A9, B2:B9, 3).

Expected Result: The function will return an array showing the top 3 most frequent customers and their visit counts.

Calculate Product Discounts

D2		▾	*fx* =CALCULATE_PRODUCT_DISCOUNTS(A2:A8, B2:B8, C2:C8)		
	A	B	C	D	E
1	Product	Original Price	Discount (%)		
2	Laptop	1000	10	Laptop	900.00
3	Smartphone	500	15	Smartphone	425.00
4	Tablet	300	5	Tablet	285.00
5	Headphones	120	20	Headphones	96.00
6	Monitor	250	8	Monitor	230.00
7	Keyboard	80	12	Keyboard	70.40
8	Mouse	50	10	Mouse	45.00

Objective: Write a function that applies a percentage discount to products and returns their discounted prices.
Sample Data:

Product	Original Price	Discount (%)
Laptop	1000	10
Smartphone	500	15
Tablet	300	5
Headphones	120	20
Monitor	250	8
Keyboard	80	12
Mouse	50	10

Learning Outcomes:
- Learn to apply percentage discounts to original prices.
- Practice arithmetic operations to calculate discounted prices.

Code Example:

```
/**
 * Calculates the discounted prices of products.
 *
 * @param {range} products The range containing product
names.
 * @param {range} prices The range containing original prices.
 * @param {range} discounts The range containing discount
percentages.
 * @return {array | string} An array listing products and their
discounted prices, or an error message if input data is invalid.
 * @customfunction
 */
function CALCULATE_PRODUCT_DISCOUNTS(products,
prices, discounts) {
const result = [];
for (let i = 0; i < products.length; i++) {
const product = products[i][0];
const price = prices[i][0];
const discount = discounts[i][0];
if (typeof product === 'string' && typeof price === 'number'
&& typeof discount === 'number' && discount >= 0 &&
discount <= 100) {
const finalPrice = price - (price * (discount / 100));
result.push([product, finalPrice.toFixed(2)]);
}
}
return result.length > 0 ? result : "Invalid or empty data!";
}
```

Steps:
1. Paste the code into a new Apps Script project.
2. Save the changes and return to Google Sheets.
3. Enter the sample data into columns A1:C8.
4. Use the function like
   =CALCULATE_PRODUCT_DISCOUNTS(A2:A8,
   B2:B8, C2:C8).

Expected Result: The function will return an array showing
each product with its discounted price.

List Projects by Department

Objective: Write a function that lists the projects assigned to each department.

Sample Data:

Department	Project
Marketing	Market Analysis
Sales	Client Outreach
IT	Infrastructure Upgrade
HR	Recruitment Plan
Sales	Sales Pipeline
Marketing	Campaign Planning
IT	Software Upgrade
HR	Employee Training

Learning Outcomes:
- Learn to group projects by department.
- Practice data filtering and grouping to match departments.

Code Example:

```
/**
* Lists the projects assigned to each department.
*
* @param {range} departments The range containing
department names.
* @param {range} projects The range containing project
names.
```

```
 * @return {array | string} An array with departments and
their projects, or an error message if input data is invalid.
 * @customfunction
 */
function PROJECTS_BY_DEPARTMENT(departments,
projects) {
 const departmentProjects = {};
 for (let i = 0; i < departments.length; i++) {
 const department = departments[i][0];
 const project = projects[i][0];
 if (typeof department === 'string' && typeof project ===
'string') {
 if (!departmentProjects[department])
departmentProjects[department] = [];
 departmentProjects[department].push(project);
 }
 }
 const result =
Object.entries(departmentProjects).map(([department,
projectList]) => [department, projectList.join(', ')]);
 return result.length > 0 ? result : "No valid data!";
}
```

Steps:

1. Paste the code into a new Apps Script project.
2. Save the changes and return to Google Sheets.
3. Enter the sample data into columns A1:B9.
4. Use the function like
   =PROJECTS_BY_DEPARTMENT(A2:A9, B2:B9).

Expected Result: The function will return an array listing departments and their associated projects.

Identify Most Common Feedback Keywords

C2	▾	fx =COMMON_FEEDBACK_KEYWORDS(A2:A8, B2:B8)		
	A	B	C	D
1	Customer	Feedback		
2	Alice	Great service, quick delivery	quick	3
3	Bob	Slow response, good prices	delivery	3
4	Carol	Helpful support, but shipping was delayed	prices	3
5	David	Quick delivery, great support	support	3
6	Emily	Prices are high, but service is excellent	great	2
7	Frank	Delivery was delayed, support is helpful	service	2
8	Helen	Excellent prices and quick shipping	helpful	2
9			shipping	2
10			delayed	2
11			excellent	2
12			slow	1
13			response	1
14			good	1
15			high	1

Objective: Write a function to identify the most common keywords in customer feedback comments.

Sample Data:

Customer	Feedback
Alice	Great service, quick delivery
Bob	Slow response, good prices
Carol	Helpful support, but shipping was delayed
David	Quick delivery, great support
Emily	Prices are high, but service is excellent
Frank	Delivery was delayed, support is helpful
Helen	Excellent prices and quick shipping

Learning Outcomes:
- Learn to process and analyze text data to extract common keywords.
- Practice working with string methods and regular expressions.

Code Example:

```
/**
 * Identifies the most common keywords in customer
feedback comments.
 *
 * @param {range} customers The range containing customer
names.
```

```
 * @param {range} feedback The range containing feedback
comments.
 * @return {array | string} An array listing the most common
keywords and their counts, or an error message if input data
is invalid.
 * @customfunction
 */
function COMMON_FEEDBACK_KEYWORDS(customers,
feedback) {
const wordCounts = {};
const stopwords = ['the', 'and', 'is', 'are', 'was', 'were', 'but', 'a',
'an', 'to', 'of', 'for'];
feedback.flat().forEach(comment => {
if (typeof comment === 'string') {
const words = comment.toLowerCase().replace(/[^a-z\s]/g,
'').split(/\s+/);
words.forEach(word => {
if (word && !stopwords.includes(word)) {
wordCounts[word] = (wordCounts[word] || 0) + 1;
}
});
}
});
const result = Object.entries(wordCounts).map(([word,
count]) => [word, count]).sort((a, b) => b[1] - a[1]);
return result.length > 0 ? result : "No valid keywords found!";
}
```

Steps:
1. Paste the code into a new Apps Script project.
2. Save the changes and return to Google Sheets.
3. Enter the sample data into columns A1:B8.
4. Use the function like
    =COMMON_FEEDBACK_KEYWORDS(A2:A8,
    B2:B8).

Expected Result: The function will return an array listing the
most common feedback keywords and their occurrence
counts.

Track Monthly Revenue per Salesperson

D2	▼	fx	=MONTHLY_REVENUE_PER_SALESPERSON(A2:A10, B2:B10, C2:C10)	
	A	B	C	D	E
1	Salesperson	Month	Revenue		
2	Alice	January	12000	Alice - January	12000.00
3	Bob	January	15000	Bob - January	15000.00
4	Carol	January	18000	Carol - January	18000.00
5	Alice	February	10000	Alice - February	10000.00
6	Bob	February	16000	Bob - February	16000.00
7	Carol	February	14000	Carol - February	14000.00
8	Alice	March	13000	Alice - March	13000.00
9	Bob	March	17000	Bob - March	17000.00
10	Carol	March	15000	Carol - March	15000.00

Objective: Write a function to calculate the total monthly revenue generated by each salesperson.

Sample Data:

Salesperson	Month	Revenue
Alice	January	12000
Bob	January	15000
Carol	January	18000
Alice	February	10000
Bob	February	16000
Carol	February	14000
Alice	March	13000
Bob	March	17000
Carol	March	15000

Learning Outcomes:
- Learn to aggregate revenue data by salesperson and month.
- Practice grouping and summing data by multiple columns.

Code Example:
```
/**
```

* Calculates the monthly revenue generated by each salesperson.
*
* @param {range} salespeople The range containing salesperson names.
* @param {range} months The range containing month names.
* @param {range} revenues The range containing revenue data.
* @return {array | string} An array with salespeople and their monthly revenues, or an error message if input data is invalid.
* @customfunction
*/

```
function
MONTHLY_REVENUE_PER_SALESPERSON(salespeople,
months, revenues) {
const revenueData = {};
for (let i = 0; i < salespeople.length; i++) {
const salesperson = salespeople[i][0];
const month = months[i][0];
const revenue = revenues[i][0];
if (typeof salesperson === 'string' && typeof month ===
'string' && typeof revenue === 'number') {
const key = salesperson + ' - ' + month;
revenueData[key] = (revenueData[key] || 0) + revenue;
}
}
const result = Object.entries(revenueData).map(([key, total])
=> [key, total.toFixed(2)]);
return result.length > 0 ? result : "No valid data!";
}
```

Steps:
1. Paste the code into a new Apps Script project.
2. Save the changes and return to Google Sheets.
3. Enter the sample data into columns A1:C10.

4. Use the function like
=MONTHLY_REVENUE_PER_SALESPERSON(A2:A
10, B2:B10, C2:C10).

Expected Result: The function will return an array listing each salesperson's monthly revenue.

Elapsed Time Between Start and End Dates

D2	▾	fx =TASK_DURATION_IN_DAYS(A2:A7, B2:B7, C2:C7)				
	A	B	C	D	E
1	Task	Start Date	End Date		
2	Task A	2024-01-01	2024-01-10	Task A	9 days
3	Task B	2024-02-05	2024-02-15	Task B	10 days
4	Task C	2024-03-01	2024-03-07	Task C	6 days
5	Task D	2024-04-12	2024-04-18	Task D	6 days
6	Task E	2024-05-03	2024-05-09	Task E	6 days
7	Task F	2024-06-15	2024-06-20	Task F	5 days

Objective: Write a function to calculate the number of days between start and end dates for tasks.

Sample Data:

Task	Start Date	End Date
Task A	2024-01-01	2024-01-10
Task B	2024-02-05	2024-02-15
Task C	2024-03-01	2024-03-07
Task D	2024-04-12	2024-04-18
Task E	2024-05-03	2024-05-09
Task F	2024-06-15	2024-06-20

Learning Outcomes:
- Learn to work with JavaScript Date objects to calculate elapsed time.
- Understand date arithmetic to calculate differences in days.

Code Example:
/**

* Calculates the number of days between the start and end
dates for tasks.
*

* @param {range} tasks The range containing task names.
* @param {range} startDates The range containing start dates
for each task.
* @param {range} endDates The range containing end dates
for each task.
* @return {array | string} An array listing tasks and their
durations in days, or an error message if input data is invalid.
* @customfunction
*/

```
function TASK_DURATION_IN_DAYS(tasks, startDates,
endDates) {
const result = [];
for (let i = 0; i < tasks.length; i++) {
const task = tasks[i][0];
const startDate = new Date(startDates[i][0]);
const endDate = new Date(endDates[i][0]);
if (typeof task === 'string' && !isNaN(startDate) &&
!isNaN(endDate) && startDate <= endDate) {
const durationInDays = Math.floor((endDate - startDate) /
(1000 * 60 * 60 * 24));
result.push([task, durationInDays + ' days']);
}
}
return result.length > 0 ? result : "Invalid or empty data!";
}
```

Steps:
1. Paste the code into a new Apps Script project.
2. Save the changes and return to Google Sheets.
3. Enter the sample data into columns A1:C7.
4. Use the function like
   =TASK_DURATION_IN_DAYS(A2:A7, B2:B7, C2:C7).

Expected Result: The function will return an array listing
tasks and their durations in days.

Calculate Percentage Distribution by Region

C2	▼	*fx* =PERCENTAGE_DISTRIBUTION_BY_REGION(A2:A5, B2:B5)			
	A	B	C	D	E
1	Region	Sales			
2	East	3000	East	23.08%	
3	West	2500	West	19.23%	
4	North	4000	North	30.77%	
5	South	3500	South	26.92%	

Objective: Write a function that calculates the percentage distribution of total sales by region.

Sample Data:

Region	Sales
East	3000
West	2500
North	4000
South	3500

Learning Outcomes:
- Learn to calculate percentages relative to a total.
- Practice using arithmetic operations to compute proportion.

Code Example:

```
/**
* Calculates the percentage distribution of sales by region.
*
* @param {range} regions The range containing region
names.
* @param {range} sales The range containing sales values for
each region.
* @return {array | string} An array with regions and their
percentage distribution, or an error message if input data is
invalid.
* @customfunction
*/
```

```
function
PERCENTAGE_DISTRIBUTION_BY_REGION(regions, sales)
{
  const totalSales = sales.flat().reduce((sum, value) => typeof
value === 'number' ? sum + value : sum, 0);
  if (totalSales === 0) return "No valid sales data!";
  const result = regions.map((region, index) => {
  const sale = sales[index][0];
  if (typeof sale === 'number') {
  return [region[0], ((sale / totalSales) * 100).toFixed(2) + '%'];
  }
  return [region[0], "Invalid data"];
  });
  return result.length > 0 ? result : "Invalid or empty data!";
}
```

Steps:

1. Paste the code into a new Apps Script project.
2. Save the changes and return to Google Sheets.
3. Enter the sample data into columns A1:B5.
4. Use the function like
   =PERCENTAGE_DISTRIBUTION_BY_REGION(A2:A5, B2:B5).

Expected Result: The function will return an array listing regions and their percentage of total sales.

Min and Max Temperatures per Month

C2 | ▾ | fx =MIN_MAX_TEMPERATURES_PER_MONTH(A2:A9, B2:B9)

	A	B	C	D	E
1	Date	Temperature			
2	2024-01-01	5	2024-01	5°C	7°C
3	2024-01-05	7	2024-02	10°C	12°C
4	2024-02-01	10	2024-03	15°C	18°C
5	2024-02-15	12	2024-04	20°C	22°C
6	2024-03-01	15			
7	2024-03-10	18			
8	2024-04-01	20			
9	2024-04-20	22			

Objective: Write a function to identify the minimum and maximum temperatures recorded for each month.

Sample Data:

Date	Temperature
2024-01-01	5
2024-01-05	7
2024-02-01	10
2024-02-15	12
2024-03-01	15
2024-03-10	18
2024-04-01	20
2024-04-20	22

Learning Outcomes:
- Learn to group and aggregate data by month.
- Practice identifying the minimum and maximum values within a group.

Code Example:

```
/**
 * Identifies the minimum and maximum temperatures for
each month.
 *
 * @param {range} dates The range containing the dates.
 * @param {range} temperatures The range containing
temperature readings.
 * @return {array | string} An array listing months with their
minimum and maximum temperatures, or an error message if
input data is invalid.
 * @customfunction
 */
function MIN_MAX_TEMPERATURES_PER_MONTH(dates,
temperatures) {
 const monthlyTemps = {};
for (let i = 0; i < dates.length; i++) {
```

```
const date = new Date(dates[i][0]);
const temp = temperatures[i][0];
if (!isNaN(date) && typeof temp === 'number') {
const monthYear = date.toISOString().slice(0, 7);
if (!monthlyTemps[monthYear]) monthlyTemps[monthYear]
= { min: temp, max: temp };
monthlyTemps[monthYear].min =
Math.min(monthlyTemps[monthYear].min, temp);
monthlyTemps[monthYear].max =
Math.max(monthlyTemps[monthYear].max, temp);
}
}
const result =
Object.entries(monthlyTemps).map(([monthYear, data]) => [
monthYear, data.min + "°C", data.max + "°C"
]);
return result.length > 0 ? result : "No valid data!";
}
```

Steps:

1. Paste the code into a new Apps Script project.
2. Save the changes and return to Google Sheets.
3. Enter the sample data into columns A1:B9.
4. Use the function like
   =MIN_MAX_TEMPERATURES_PER_MONTH(A2:A
   9, B2:B9).

Expected Result: The function will return an array listing months with their minimum and maximum temperatures.

Calculate Cumulative Savings Over Time

C2	▾	f_x =CUMULATIVE_SAVINGS_OVER_TIME(A2:A8, B2:B8)	

	A	B	C	D
1	Month	Deposit		
2	January	500	January	500.00
3	February	600	February	1100.00
4	March	450	March	1550.00
5	April	700	April	2250.00
6	May	800	May	3050.00
7	June	650	June	3700.00
8	July	900	July	4600.00

Objective: Write a function to calculate cumulative savings over time based on monthly deposits.

Sample Data:

Month	Deposit
January	500
February	600
March	450
April	700
May	800
June	650
July	900

Learning Outcomes:
- Learn to compute cumulative sums for financial data.
- Practice using arithmetic operations to aggregate cumulative savings.

Code Example:
```
/**
 * Calculates the cumulative savings over time based on
monthly deposits.
 *
 * @param {range} months The range containing month
names.
```

```
 * @param {range} deposits The range containing monthly
deposit amounts.
 * @return {array | string} An array listing months and their
cumulative savings, or an error message if input data is
invalid.
 * @customfunction
 */
function CUMULATIVE_SAVINGS_OVER_TIME(months,
deposits) {
let cumulativeSavings = 0;
const result = [];
for (let i = 0; i < months.length; i++) {
const month = months[i][0];
const deposit = deposits[i][0];
if (typeof month === 'string' && typeof deposit ===
'number') {
cumulativeSavings += deposit;
result.push([month, cumulativeSavings.toFixed(2)]);
}
}
return result.length > 0 ? result : "Invalid or empty data!";
}
```

Steps:

1. Paste the code into a new Apps Script project.
2. Save the changes and return to Google Sheets.
3. Enter the sample data into columns A1:B8.
4. Use the function like
   =CUMULATIVE_SAVINGS_OVER_TIME(A2:A8,
   B2:B8).

Expected Result: The function will return an array showing each month and the cumulative savings up to that point.

Categorize Expenses into Ranges

C2	▼	fx =CATEGORIZE_EXPENSES_BY_RANGE(A2:A8, B2:B8)	

	A	B	C	D
1	Expense	Amount		
2	Rent	1200	Rent	High (> 500)
3	Groceries	350	Groceries	Medium (101 - 500)
4	Utilities	150	Utilities	Medium (101 - 500)
5	Transport	60	Transport	Low (<= 100)
6	Dining Out	80	Dining Out	Low (<= 100)
7	Entertainment	100	Entertainment	Low (<= 100)
8	Insurance	400	Insurance	Medium (101 - 500)

Objective: Write a function that categorizes each expense into a specific range based on its value.

Sample Data:

Expense	Amount
Rent	1200
Groceries	350
Utilities	150
Transport	60
Dining Out	80
Entertainment	100
Insurance	400

Learning Outcomes:
- Practice categorizing numerical data into predefined ranges.
- Learn to apply conditional logic to map each value to a range.

Code Example:

```
/**
 * Categorizes expenses into specified ranges.
 *
 * @param {range} expenses The range containing expense
names.
```

```
 * @param {range} amounts The range containing expense
amounts.
 * @return {array | string} An array listing expenses and their
respective ranges, or an error message if input data is invalid.
 * @customfunction
 */
function CATEGORIZE_EXPENSES_BY_RANGE(expenses,
amounts) {
function findRange(amount) {
if (amount <= 100) return 'Low (<= 100)';
else if (amount <= 500) return 'Medium (101 - 500)';
else return 'High (> 500)';
}
const result = expenses.map((expense, index) => {
const amount = amounts[index][0];
if (typeof amount === 'number') {
return [expense[0], findRange(amount)];
}
return [expense[0], "Invalid amount"];
});
return result.length > 0 ? result : "Invalid or empty data!";
}
```

Steps:

1. Paste the code into a new Apps Script project.
2. Save the changes and return to Google Sheets.
3. Enter the sample data into columns A1:B8.
4. Use the function like
   =CATEGORIZE_EXPENSES_BY_RANGE(A2:A8,
   B2:B8).

Expected Result: The function will return an array showing each expense and its categorized range.

Calculate Average Monthly Rainfall

	A	B	C	D
C2		▼	fx =AVERAGE_MONTHLY_RAINFALL(A2:A10, B2:B10)	
1	Date	Rainfall (mm)		
2	2024-01-01	5	2024-01	8.33 mm
3	2024-01-02	8	2024-02	15.00 mm
4	2024-01-03	12	2024-03	8.00 mm
5	2024-02-01	15		
6	2024-02-02	10		
7	2024-02-03	20		
8	2024-03-01	7		
9	2024-03-02	5		
10	2024-03-03	12		

Objective: Write a function to calculate the average monthly rainfall from daily data.

Sample Data:

Date	Rainfall (mm)
2024-01-01	5
2024-01-02	8
2024-01-03	12
2024-02-01	15
2024-02-02	10
2024-02-03	20
2024-03-01	7
2024-03-02	5
2024-03-03	12

Learning Outcomes:
- Learn to group and aggregate daily data into monthly averages.
- Practice calculating averages using arithmetic operations.

Code Example:

```
/**
 * Calculates the average monthly rainfall from daily data.
 *
 * @param {range} dates The range containing date values.
 * @param {range} rainfall The range containing daily rainfall
data.
 * @return {array | string} An array listing months and their
average rainfall, or an error message if input data is invalid.
 * @customfunction
 */
function AVERAGE_MONTHLY_RAINFALL(dates, rainfall)
{
const monthlyData = {};
for (let i = 0; i < dates.length; i++) {
const date = new Date(dates[i][0]);
const rain = rainfall[i][0];
if (!isNaN(date) && typeof rain === 'number') {
const monthYear = date.toISOString().slice(0, 7);
if (!monthlyData[monthYear]) monthlyData[monthYear] = {
sum: 0, count: 0 };
monthlyData[monthYear].sum += rain;
monthlyData[monthYear].count++;
}
}
const result =
Object.entries(monthlyData).map(([monthYear, data]) => [
monthYear, (data.sum / data.count).toFixed(2) + ' mm'
]);
return result.length > 0 ? result : "No valid data!";
}
```

Steps:

1. Paste the code into a new Apps Script project.
2. Save the changes and return to Google Sheets.
3. Enter the sample data into columns A1:B10.
4. Use the function like
   =AVERAGE_MONTHLY_RAINFALL(A2:A10,
   B2:B10).

Expected Result: The function will return an array listing each month with its average rainfall.

Identify Employees with Long Tenure

C2	▼	fx =LONG_TENURE_EMPLOYEES(A2:A8, B2:B8, 10)		
	A	B	C	D
1	Employee	Hire Date		
2	Alice	2010-01-05	Alice	14 years
3	Bob	2014-07-15	David	15 years
4	Carol	2016-03-20	Emily	11 years
5	David	2008-09-12	George	13 years
6	Emily	2012-11-30		
7	Frank	2018-05-25		
8	George	2011-02-17		

Objective: Write a function that identifies employees who have been with the company for more than a specified number of years.

Sample Data:

Employee	Hire Date
Alice	2010-01-05
Bob	2014-07-15
Carol	2016-03-20
David	2008-09-12
Emily	2012-11-30
Frank	2018-05-25
George	2011-02-17

Learning Outcomes:
- Learn to calculate tenure based on the current date and hire date.
- Understand how to compare years and filter results conditionally.

Code Example:

```
/**
 * Identifies employees who have been with the company for
 more than the specified number of years.
 *
 * @param {range} employees The range containing employee
 names.
 * @param {range} hireDates The range containing hire dates
 of each employee.
 * @param {number} minYears The minimum number of
 years required for long tenure.
 * @return {array | string} An array listing employees with
 long tenure, or an error message if input data is invalid.
 * @customfunction
 */
function LONG_TENURE_EMPLOYEES(employees,
hireDates, minYears) {
if (typeof minYears !== 'number' || minYears <= 0) return
"Invalid value for minimum years";
const today = new Date();
const result = [];
for (let i = 0; i < employees.length; i++) {
const hireDate = new Date(hireDates[i][0]);
if (!isNaN(hireDate)) {
let tenureYears = today.getFullYear() -
hireDate.getFullYear();
if (today.getMonth() < hireDate.getMonth() ||
(today.getMonth() === hireDate.getMonth() &&
today.getDate() < hireDate.getDate())) {
tenureYears--;
}
if (tenureYears >= minYears) {
result.push([employees[i][0], tenureYears + ' years']);
}
}
}
return result.length > 0 ? result : "No employees found with
long tenure!";
```

}
Steps:
1. Paste the code into a new Apps Script project.
2. Save the changes and return to Google Sheets.
3. Enter the sample data into columns A1:B8.
4. Use the function like
   =LONG_TENURE_EMPLOYEES(A2:A8, B2:B8, 10).

Expected Result: The function will return an array listing employees with a tenure of 10 or more years.

8 : Interactive Sheet Functions

Explore the interactive possibilities of Google Sheets by creating custom functions that respond to user input and changes within the sheet.

Calculate Weekly Revenue Growth

C2	▼	*fx* =WEEKLY_REVENUE_GROWTH(A2:A7, B2:B7)		
	A	B	C	D
1	Week	Revenue		
2	Week 1	2000	Week	Growth %
3	Week 2	2400	Week 2	20.00%
4	Week 3	2200	Week 3	-8.33%
5	Week 4	2600	Week 4	18.18%
6	Week 5	2500	Week 5	-3.85%
7	Week 6	2700	Week 6	8.00%

Objective: Write a function that calculates weekly revenue growth percentages.

Sample Data:

Week	Revenue
Week 1	2000
Week 2	2400
Week 3	2200
Week 4	2600
Week 5	2500
Week 6	2700

Learning Outcomes:
- Learn to calculate percentage growth between consecutive weeks.
- Practice arithmetic operations to determine the relative change.

Code Example:

```javascript
/**
 * Calculates weekly revenue growth percentages.
 *
 * @param {range} weeks The range containing week
identifiers.
 * @param {range} revenues The range containing revenue
amounts for each week.
 * @return {array | string} An array with weeks and their
growth percentages, or an error message if input data is
invalid.
 * @customfunction
 */
function WEEKLY_REVENUE_GROWTH(weeks, revenues) {
 const result = [["Week", "Growth %"]];
for (let i = 1; i < weeks.length; i++) {
 const week = weeks[i][0];
 const prevRevenue = revenues[i - 1][0];
 const currRevenue = revenues[i][0];
 if (typeof prevRevenue === 'number' && typeof
currRevenue === 'number') {
 const growth = ((currRevenue - prevRevenue) /
prevRevenue) * 100;
 result.push([week, growth.toFixed(2) + "%"]);
 } else {
 result.push([week, "Invalid data"]);
 }
 }
 return result.length > 1 ? result : "Not enough data!";
}
```

Steps:

1. Paste the code into a new Apps Script project.
2. Save the changes and return to Google Sheets.
3. Enter the sample data into columns A1:B7.
4. Use the function like
   =WEEKLY_REVENUE_GROWTH(A2:A7, B2:B7).

Expected Result: The function will return an array with each week and its corresponding revenue growth percentage.

List Top-N Items by Sales Volume

C2   ▾   _fx_ =TOP_N_ITEMS_BY_SALES_VOLUME(A2:A8, B2:B8, 3)

	A	B	C	D
1	Item	Sales Volume		
2	Laptop	150	Headphones	250
3	Phone	200	Phone	200
4	Tablet	100	Monitor	180
5	Headphones	250		
6	Monitor	180		
7	Keyboard	120		
8	Mouse	140		

Objective: Write a function that lists the top-N items by sales volume.

Sample Data:

Item	Sales Volume
Laptop	150
Phone	200
Tablet	100
Headphones	250
Monitor	180
Keyboard	120
Mouse	140

Learning Outcomes:
- Learn to sort and filter data based on numerical values.
- Practice conditional logic to identify the top-N items.

Code Example:

```
/**
* Lists the top-N items by sales volume.
*
* @param {range} items The range containing item names.
* @param {range} volumes The range containing sales
volumes for each item.
```

* @param {number} n The number of top items to return.
* @return {array | string} An array listing the top-N items and their sales volumes, or an error message if input data is invalid.
* @customfunction
*/
```
function TOP_N_ITEMS_BY_SALES_VOLUME(items,
volumes, n) {
 if (typeof n !== 'number' || n <= 0) return "Invalid value for
N";
 const data = items.map((item, index) => ({ item: item[0],
volume: volumes[index][0] }))
 .filter(entry => typeof entry.item === 'string' && typeof
entry.volume === 'number')
 .sort((a, b) => b.volume - a.volume);
 const result = data.slice(0, n).map(entry => [entry.item,
entry.volume]);
 return result.length > 0 ? result : "No valid data!";
}
```

Steps:

1. Paste the code into a new Apps Script project.
2. Save the changes and return to Google Sheets.
3. Enter the sample data into columns A1:B8.
4. Use the function like
   =TOP_N_ITEMS_BY_SALES_VOLUME(A2:A8, B2:B8, 3).

Expected Result: The function will return an array listing the top 3 items by sales volume.

Calculate Total Work Hours per Employee

D2   ▾   *fx* =TOTAL_WORK_HOURS_PER_EMPLOYEE(A2:A9, C2:C9)

	A	B	C	D	E
1	Employee	Project	Hours		
2	Alice	Project A	15	Alice	51.00
3	Bob	Project B	12	Bob	50.00
4	Alice	Project C	20	Carol	24.00
5	Carol	Project A	10		
6	Bob	Project C	18		
7	Carol	Project B	14		
8	Alice	Project B	16		
9	Bob	Project A	20		

Objective: Write a function that calculates the total work hours of each employee across multiple projects.

Sample Data:

Employee	Project	Hours
Alice	Project A	15
Bob	Project B	12
Alice	Project C	20
Carol	Project A	10
Bob	Project C	18
Carol	Project B	14
Alice	Project B	16
Bob	Project A	20

Learning Outcomes:
- Learn to group data by employee name and aggregate the total hours.
- Practice using object mapping to count and sum numerical values.

Code Example:
```
/**
 * Calculates the total work hours of each employee across multiple projects.
 *
```

```
 * @param {range} employees The range containing employee
names.
 * @param {range} hours The range containing hours spent on
projects.
 * @return {array | string} An array listing employees and their
total work hours, or an error message if input data is invalid.
 * @customfunction
 */
function
TOTAL_WORK_HOURS_PER_EMPLOYEE(employees,
hours) {
 const workHours = {};
for (let i = 0; i < employees.length; i++) {
 const employee = employees[i][0];
 const hour = hours[i][0];
 if (typeof employee === 'string' && typeof hour ===
'number') {
 workHours[employee] = (workHours[employee] || 0) +
hour;
 }
 }
 const result = Object.entries(workHours).map(([employee,
total]) => [employee, total.toFixed(2)]);
 return result.length > 0 ? result : "No valid data!";
 }
```

Steps:

1. Paste the code into a new Apps Script project.
2. Save the changes and return to Google Sheets.
3. Enter the sample data into columns A1:C9.
4. Use the function like
   =TOTAL_WORK_HOURS_PER_EMPLOYEE(A2:A9,
   C2:C9).

Expected Result: The function will return an array listing
each employee and their total work hours across projects.

Calculate Profit Percentage per Region

D2   ▾   *fx* =PROFIT_PERCENTAGE_PER_REGION(A2:A6, B2:B6, C2:C6)

	A	B	C	D	E
1	Region	Revenue	Costs		
2	East	15000	10000	East	33.33%
3	West	20000	12000	West	40.00%
4	North	25000	17000	North	32.00%
5	South	18000	14000	South	22.22%
6	Central	22000	15000	Central	31.82%

Objective: Write a function to calculate the profit percentage per region.

Sample Data:

Region	Revenue	Costs
East	15000	10000
West	20000	12000
North	25000	17000
South	18000	14000
Central	22000	15000

Learning Outcomes:
- Understand how to calculate profit percentages using revenue and cost data.
- Practice using arithmetic operations to determine profit percentages.

Code Example:

```
/**
 * Calculates the profit percentage per region.
 *
 * @param {range} regions The range containing region names.
 * @param {range} revenues The range containing revenue amounts per region.
 * @param {range} costs The range containing cost amounts per region.
```

* @return {array | string} An array listing regions and their profit percentages, or an error message if input data is invalid.
* @customfunction
*/

```javascript
function PROFIT_PERCENTAGE_PER_REGION(regions, revenues, costs) {
 const result = [];
for (let i = 0; i < regions.length; i++) {
 const region = regions[i][0];
 const revenue = revenues[i][0];
 const cost = costs[i][0];
 if (typeof region === 'string' && typeof revenue === 'number' && typeof cost === 'number') {
 const profit = revenue - cost;
 const profitPercentage = ((profit / revenue) * 100).toFixed(2);
 result.push([region, profitPercentage + "%"]);
 } else {
 result.push([region, "Invalid data"]);
 }
 }
 return result.length > 0 ? result : "No valid data!";
}
```

Steps:

1. Paste the code into a new Apps Script project.
2. Save the changes and return to Google Sheets.
3. Enter the sample data into columns A1:C6.
4. Use the function like =PROFIT_PERCENTAGE_PER_REGION(A2:A6, B2:B6, C2:C6).

Expected Result: The function will return an array listing each region and its profit percentage.

Calculate Number of Days Since Last Activity

C2	▾	*fx* =DAYS_SINCE_LAST_ACTIVITY(A2:A8, B2:B8)		
	A	B	C	D
1	User	Last Activity Date		
2	Alice	2024-01-01	Alice	144 days
3	Bob	2024-01-15	Bob	130 days
4	Carol	2024-02-01	Carol	113 days
5	David	2024-01-20	David	125 days
6	Emily	2024-02-10	Emily	104 days
7	Frank	2024-02-15	Frank	99 days
8	George	2024-02-20	George	94 days

Objective: Write a function that calculates the number of days since the last recorded activity.

Sample Data:

User	Last Activity Date
Alice	2024-01-01
Bob	2024-01-15
Carol	2024-02-01
David	2024-01-20
Emily	2024-02-10
Frank	2024-02-15
George	2024-02-20

Learning Outcomes:
- Learn to compute the difference between two dates in JavaScript.
- Understand date manipulation and arithmetic to calculate elapsed days.

Code Example:
```
/**
* Calculates the number of days since the last recorded
activity.
*
```

```
* @param {range} users The range containing user names.
* @param {range} lastActivityDates The range containing the
last activity dates.
* @return {array | string} An array listing users and their days
since the last activity, or an error message if input data is
invalid.
* @customfunction
*/
function DAYS_SINCE_LAST_ACTIVITY(users,
lastActivityDates) {
 const today = new Date();
 const result = [];
for (let i = 0; i < users.length; i++) {
 const user = users[i][0];
 const lastActivityDate = new Date(lastActivityDates[i][0]);
 if (!isNaN(lastActivityDate)) {
 const diffDays = Math.floor((today - lastActivityDate) /
(1000 * 60 * 60 * 24));
 result.push([user, diffDays + ' days']);
 } else {
 result.push([user, "Invalid date"]);
 }
 }
 return result.length > 0 ? result : "No valid data!";
}
```

Steps:

1. Paste the code into a new Apps Script project.
2. Save the changes and return to Google Sheets.
3. Enter the sample data into columns A1:B8.
4. Use the function like
   =DAYS_SINCE_LAST_ACTIVITY(A2:A8, B2:B8).

Expected Result: The function will return an array listing
users and the number of days since their last recorded
activity.

Identify Overdue Invoices

D2   ▼   ƒx =IDENTIFY_OVERDUE_INVOICES(A2:A8, B2:B8, C2:C8)

	A	B	C	D	E	F
1	Invoice	Due Date	Amount			
2	INV-001	2024-01-05	1200	INV-001	2024-01-05	1200.00
3	INV-002	2024-01-15	1500	INV-002	2024-01-15	1500.00
4	INV-003	2024-02-01	1800	INV-003	2024-02-01	1800.00
5	INV-004	2024-02-10	1000	INV-004	2024-02-10	1000.00
6	INV-005	2024-03-01	1600	INV-005	2024-03-01	1600.00
7	INV-006	2024-03-15	1400	INV-006	2024-03-15	1400.00
8	INV-007	2024-03-20	2000	INV-007	2024-03-20	2000.00

Objective: Write a function to identify overdue invoices given the due dates.

Sample Data:

Invoice	Due Date	Amount
INV-001	2024-01-05	1200
INV-002	2024-01-15	1500
INV-003	2024-02-01	1800
INV-004	2024-02-10	1000
INV-005	2024-03-01	1600
INV-006	2024-03-15	1400
INV-007	2024-03-20	2000

Learning Outcomes:
- Learn to compare due dates against the current date.
- Understand how to filter data based on overdue status.

Code Example:

```
/**
 * Identifies overdue invoices based on due dates.
 *
 * @param {range} invoices The range containing invoice
identifiers.
 * @param {range} dueDates The range containing due dates
for each invoice.
```

```
 * @param {range} amounts The range containing invoice
amounts.
 * @return {array | string} An array listing overdue invoices
and their amounts, or an error message if no overdue invoices
are found.
 * @customfunction
 */
function IDENTIFY_OVERDUE_INVOICES(invoices,
dueDates, amounts) {
 const today = new Date();
 const result = [];
for (let i = 0; i < invoices.length; i++) {
 const invoice = invoices[i][0];
 const dueDate = new Date(dueDates[i][0]);
 const amount = amounts[i][0];
 if (!isNaN(dueDate) && typeof amount === 'number' &&
dueDate < today) {
 result.push([invoice, dueDate.toISOString().split('T')[0],
amount.toFixed(2)]);
 }
 }
 return result.length > 0 ? result : "No overdue invoices
found!";
}
```

Steps:
1. Paste the code into a new Apps Script project.
2. Save the changes and return to Google Sheets.
3. Enter the sample data into columns A1:C8.
4. Use the function like
   =IDENTIFY_OVERDUE_INVOICES(A2:A8, B2:B8,
   C2:C8).

Expected Result: The function will return an array listing
overdue invoices and their amounts.

Sum of Sales by Product Category

	A	B	C	D
1	Product Category	Sales		
2	Electronics	1500	Electronics	5300
3	Clothing	800	Clothing	1300
4	Electronics	2000	Home Goods	1900
5	Home Goods	1200		
6	Clothing	500		
7	Electronics	1800		
8	Home Goods	700		

Objective: Write a function to calculate the total sales for each product category.

Sample Data:

Product Category	Sales
Electronics	1500
Clothing	800
Electronics	2000
Home Goods	1200
Clothing	500
Electronics	1800
Home Goods	700

Learning Outcomes:
- Practice grouping data by category and summing up values.
- Understand how to manipulate data to achieve aggregate results.

Code Example:

```
/**
* Calculates the total sales for each product category.
*
```

```
 * @param {range} categories The range containing product
categories.
 * @param {range} sales The range containing sales amounts.
 * @return {array | string} An array listing product categories
and their total sales, or an error message if input data is
invalid.
 * @customfunction
 */
function SUM_OF_SALES_BY_CATEGORY(categories, sales)
{
 const categorySales = {};
for (let i = 0; i < categories.length; i++) {
 const category = categories[i][0];
 const sale = sales[i][0];
 if (typeof category === 'string' && typeof sale === 'number')
{
categorySales[category] = (categorySales[category] || 0) +
sale;
 }
 }
 const result = Object.entries(categorySales).map(([category,
total]) => [category, total]);
 return result.length > 0 ? result : "No valid data!";
}
```

Steps:

1. Paste the code into a new Apps Script project.
2. Save the changes and return to Google Sheets.
3. Enter the sample data into columns A1:B8.
4. Use the function like
   =SUM_OF_SALES_BY_CATEGORY(A2:A8, B2:B8).

Expected Result: The function will return an array listing
each product category along with the total sales.

Identify High Performing Employees

▾   ƒx =HIGH_PERFORMING_EMPLOYEES(A2:A8, B2:B8, 85)

	A	B	C	D
1	Employee	Performance Rating		
2	Alice	85	Bob	95
3	Bob	95	David	90
4	Carol	75	Emily	88
5	David	90	George	92
6	Emily	88		
7	Frank	80		
8	George	92		

Objective: Write a function to identify employees whose performance ratings exceed a certain threshold.

Sample Data:

Employee	Performance Rating
Alice	85
Bob	95
Carol	75
David	90
Emily	88
Frank	80
George	92

Learning Outcomes:
- Learn to filter data based on numerical thresholds.
- Practice extracting relevant information through conditional statements.

Code Example:

```
/**
 * Identifies high performing employees based on a
performing rating threshold.
 *
```

```
 * @param {range} employees The range containing employee
names.
 * @param {range} ratings The range containing performance
ratings.
 * @param {number} threshold The performance rating
threshold.
 * @return {array | string} An array listing employees who
exceed the performance threshold, or an error message if no
employees meet the criteria.
 * @customfunction
 */
function HIGH_PERFORMING_EMPLOYEES(employees,
ratings, threshold) {
 const result = [];
for (let i = 0; i < employees.length; i++) {
 const employee = employees[i][0];
 const rating = ratings[i][0];
 if (typeof rating === 'number' && rating > threshold) {
 result.push([employee, rating]);
 }
 }
 return result.length > 0 ? result : "No high performing
employees found!";
}
```

Steps:

1. Paste the code into a new Apps Script project.
2. Save the changes and return to Google Sheets.
3. Enter the sample data into columns A1:B8.
4. Use the function like
   =HIGH_PERFORMING_EMPLOYEES(A2:A8, B2:B8,
   85).

Expected Result: The function will return an array listing
employees whose performance ratings are above 85.

Track Days Since Last Purchase

	A	B	C	D
1	Customer	Last Purchase Date		
2	Alice	2024-01-05	Alice	140 days
3	Bob	2024-02-10	Bob	104 days
4	Carol	2024-02-15	Carol	99 days
5	David	2024-03-01	David	84 days
6	Emily	2024-03-20	Emily	66 days
7	Frank	2024-04-05	Frank	50 days
8	George	2024-04-18	George	37 days

Objective: Write a function to calculate the number of days since each customer's last purchase.

Sample Data:

Customer	Last Purchase Date
Alice	2024-01-05
Bob	2024-02-10
Carol	2024-02-15
David	2024-03-01
Emily	2024-03-20
Frank	2024-04-05
George	2024-04-18

Learning Outcomes:
- Learn to calculate the time difference between dates.
- Understand how to use dates to monitor customer activity.

Code Example:
```
/**
 * Calculates the number of days since each customer's last purchase.
 *
```

```
 * @param {range} customers The range containing customer
names.
 * @param {range} lastPurchaseDates The range containing
the last purchase dates for each customer.
 * @return {array | string} An array listing customers and the
number of days since their last purchase, or an error message
if input data is invalid.
 * @customfunction
 */
function DAYS_SINCE_LAST_PURCHASE(customers,
lastPurchaseDates) {
 const today = new Date();
 const result = [];
for (let i = 0; i < customers.length; i++) {
 const customer = customers[i][0];
 const lastPurchaseDate = new Date(lastPurchaseDates[i][0]);
 if (!isNaN(lastPurchaseDate)) {
 const daysSince = Math.floor((today - lastPurchaseDate) /
(1000 * 60 * 60 * 24));
 result.push([customer, daysSince + ' days']);
 } else {
 result.push([customer, "Invalid date"]);
 }
 }
 return result.length > 0 ? result : "No valid data!";
 }
```

Steps:

1. Paste the code into a new Apps Script project.
2. Save the changes and return to Google Sheets.
3. Enter the sample data into columns A1:B8.
4. Use the function like
   =DAYS_SINCE_LAST_PURCHASE(A2:A8, B2:B8).

Expected Result: The function will return an array listing
each customer and the number of days since their last
purchase.

Calculate Weighted Average Score

D2	▾	ƒx =WEIGHTED_AVERAGE_SCORE(A2:A4, B2:B4, C2:C4)		
	A	B	C	D
1	Assessment	Score	Weight (%)	
2	Quiz	85	20	88.00
3	Project	90	30	
4	Final Exam	88	50	

Objective: Write a function to calculate the weighted average score for a set of assessments.

Sample Data:

Assessment	Score	Weight (%)
Quiz	85	20
Project	90	30
Final Exam	88	50

Learning Outcomes:
- Practice calculating weighted averages, a common statistical calculation.
- Understand the importance of weightings in average calculations.

Code Example:

```
/**
* Calculates the weighted average score for assessments.
*
* @param {range} assessments The range containing assessment names.
* @param {range} scores The range containing scores.
* @param {range} weights The range containing weights in percentage.
* @return {number | string} The weighted average score or an error message if input data is invalid.
* @customfunction
*/
function WEIGHTED_AVERAGE_SCORE(assessments, scores, weights) {
```

```
const totalWeightedScore = 0;
const totalWeight = 0;
for (let i = 0; i < assessments.length; i++) {
const score = scores[i][0];
const weight = weights[i][0];
if (typeof score === 'number' && typeof weight ===
'number') {
totalWeightedScore += score * (weight / 100);
totalWeight += weight;
}
}
if (totalWeight === 100) {
return totalWeightedScore.toFixed(2);
} else {
return "Weights do not sum up to 100%";
}
}
```

Steps:
1. Paste the code into a new Apps Script project.
2. Save the changes and return to Google Sheets.
3. Enter the sample data into columns A1:C4.
4. Use the function like
   =WEIGHTED_AVERAGE_SCORE(A2:A4, B2:B4,
   C2:C4).

Expected Result: The function will return the weighted average score of 88.70 if calculated correctly.

Identify Products Below Restock Level

D2	▼	f_x =PRODUCTS_BELOW_RESTOCK_LEVEL(A2:A6, B2:B6, C2:C6)		
	A	B	C	D	E
1	Product	Current Stock	Restock Level		
2	Pen	150	200	Pen	150
3	Notebook	50	100	Notebook	50
4	Eraser	300	250	Backpack	45
5	Marker	80	75		
6	Backpack	45	50		

Objective: Write a function to identify products that are below a certain restock level and need replenishment.

Sample Data:

Product	Current Stock	Restock Level
Pen	150	200
Notebook	50	100
Eraser	300	250
Marker	80	75
Backpack	45	50

Learning Outcomes:
- Learn to compare current stock levels against minimum required levels.
- Practice filtering data based on specific criteria.

Code Example:

```
/**
 * Identifies products that are below restock level.
 *
 * @param {range} products The range containing product
names.
 * @param {range} currentStocks The range containing current
stock quantities.
 * @param {range} restockLevels The range containing restock
level quantities.
 * @return {array | string} An array listing products that need
restocking, or an error message if no products need
restocking.
 * @customfunction
 */
function PRODUCTS_BELOW_RESTOCK_LEVEL(products,
currentStocks, restockLevels) {
const result = [];
for (let i = 0; i < products.length; i++) {
const product = products[i][0];
const currentStock = currentStocks[i][0];
const restockLevel = restockLevels[i][0];
```

```
if (typeof currentStock === 'number' && typeof restockLevel
=== 'number' && currentStock < restockLevel) {
result.push([product, currentStock]);
}
}
return result.length > 0 ? result : "No products below restock
level.";
}
```

Steps:

1. Paste the code into a new Apps Script project.
2. Save the changes and return to Google Sheets.
3. Enter the sample data into columns A1:C6.
4. Use the function like
   =PRODUCTS_BELOW_RESTOCK_LEVEL(A2:A6,
   B2:B6, C2:C6).

Expected Result: The function will return an array listing the products below their respective restock levels, like "Notebook" and "Backpack".

9 : Advanced Data Manipulation Techniques

Delve into advanced data manipulation techniques that help you handle larger datasets efficiently.

Calculate Total Discounts Given

D2		fx =TOTAL_DISCOUNTS_GIVEN(A2:A6, B2:B6, C2:C6)		
	A	B	C	D
1	Product	Original Price	Discounted Price	
2	T-shirt	20	15	45
3	Jeans	50	45	
4	Sweater	60	50	
5	Jacket	100	80	
6	Hat	25	20	

Objective: Write a function to calculate the total amount of discounts given based on the original prices and discounted prices.

Sample Data:

Product	Original Price	Discounted Price
T-shirt	20	15
Jeans	50	45
Sweater	60	50
Jacket	100	80
Hat	25	20

Learning Outcomes:
- Learn to calculate the difference between original and discounted prices.

208

- Understand how to aggregate savings across multiple items.

Code Example:

```
/**
 * Calculates the total discounts given.
 *
 * @param {range} products The range containing product names.
 * @param {range} originalPrices The range containing original prices.
 * @param {range} discountedPrices The range containing discounted prices.
 * @return {number|string} The total amount of discounts given or an error message if input data is invalid.
 * @customfunction
 */
function TOTAL_DISCOUNTS_GIVEN(products, originalPrices, discountedPrices) {
  let totalDiscount = 0;
  for (let i = 0; i < products.length; i++) {
    const originalPrice = originalPrices[i][0];
    const discountedPrice = discountedPrices[i][0];
    if (typeof originalPrice === 'number' && typeof discountedPrice === 'number') {
      totalDiscount += originalPrice - discountedPrice;
    }
  }
  return totalDiscount > 0 ? totalDiscount : "No discounts given or invalid data.";
}
```

Steps:

1. Paste the code into a new Apps Script project.
2. Save the changes and return to Google Sheets.

3. Enter the sample data into columns A1:C6.
4. Use the function like
   =TOTAL_DISCOUNTS_GIVEN(A2:A6, B2:B6, C2:C6).

Expected Result: The function will return the total amount of discounts given across all products.

Monitor Project Deadline Compliance

C2		fx =MONITOR_PROJECT_DEADLINES(A2:A6, B2:B6)		
	A	B	C	D
1	Project	Deadline		
2	Project A	2024-05-01	Project A	
3	Project B	2024-06-15	Project C	
4	Project C	2024-04-20	Project D	
5	Project D	2024-05-10	Project E	
6	Project E	2024-05-25		

Objective: Develop a function to monitor and report projects that are overdue based on their deadlines.

Sample Data:

Project	Deadline
Project A	2024-05-01
Project B	2024-06-15
Project C	2024-04-20
Project D	2024-05-10
Project E	2024-05-25

Learning Outcomes:
- Learn to compare dates to determine if deadlines are met.
- Practice filtering data based on a condition (current date vs deadline).

Code Example:

```
/**
 * Monitors project deadlines and reports overdue
projects.
 *
 * @param {range} projects The range containing project
names.
 * @param {range} deadlines The range containing
project deadlines.
 * @return {array | string} An array listing overdue
projects or an error message if no overdue projects are
found.
 * @customfunction
 */
function MONITOR_PROJECT_DEADLINES(projects,
deadlines) {
 const today = new Date();
 const result = [];
 for (let i = 0; i < projects.length; i++) {
 const project = projects[i][0];
 const deadline = new Date(deadlines[i][0]);
 if (!isNaN(deadline) && deadline < today) {
 result.push([project]);
 }
 }
 return result.length > 0 ? result : "No overdue projects
found.";
}
```

Steps:

1. Paste the code into a new Apps Script project.
2. Save the changes and return to Google Sheets.
3. Enter the sample data into columns A1:B6.

4. Use the function like
   =MONITOR_PROJECT_DEADLINES(A2:A6,
   B2:B6).

Expected Result: The function will return an array listing any projects that are overdue.

Calculate Employee Bonus Based on Performance

D2	▼	fx =CALCULATE_BONUS(A2:A6, B2:B6, C2:C6)			
	A	B	C	D	E
1	Employee	Performance Rating	Base Salary		
2	Alice	5	50000	Alice	62500.00
3	Bob	4	60000	Bob	72000.00
4	Carol	3	55000	Carol	63250.00
5	David	2	48000	David	52800.00
6	Emily	1	62000	Emily	65100.00

Objective: Write a function to calculate an employee's annual bonus based on their performance rating.
Sample Data:

Employee	Performance Rating	Base Salary
Alice	5	50000
Bob	4	60000
Carol	3	55000
David	2	48000
Emily	1	62000

Learning Outcomes:
- Learn to apply conditional logic to calculate bonuses based on performance ratings.
- Practice using arithmetic operations to compute final salaries.

Code Example:

```
/**
 * Calculates annual bonus based on performance rating.
 *
 * @param {range} employees The range containing
employee names.
 * @param {range} ratings The range containing
performance ratings.
 * @param {range} salaries The range containing base
salaries.
 * @return {array | string} An array listing employees
with their final salary including bonus or an error
message if input data is invalid.
 * @customfunction
 */
function CALCULATE_BONUS(employees, ratings,
salaries) {
const bonusRates = [0, 0.05, 0.10, 0.15, 0.20, 0.25];
const result = [];
for (let i = 0; i < employees.length; i++) {
const employee = employees[i][0];
const rating = ratings[i][0];
const salary = salaries[i][0];
if (typeof rating === 'number' && typeof salary ===
'number' && rating >= 1 && rating <= 5) {
const bonus = salary * bonusRates[rating];
result.push([employee, (salary + bonus).toFixed(2)]);
} else {
result.push([employee, "Invalid data"]);
}
}
return result.length > 0 ? result : "No valid data found.";
}
```

Steps:

1. Paste the code into a new Apps Script project.
2. Save the changes and return to Google Sheets.
3. Enter the sample data into columns A1:C6.
4. Use the function like
   =CALCULATE_BONUS(A2:A6, B2:B6, C2:C6).

Expected Result: The function will return an array listing each employee with their final salary after applying the bonus.

Summarize Monthly Attendance

D2	▾	*fx* =MONTHLY_ATTENDANCE_SUMMARY(A2:A7, B2:B7, C2:C7)			
	A	B	C	D	E
1	Employee	Date	Status		
2	Alice	2024-01-01	Present	Alice	2
3	Bob	2024-01-01	Absent	Carol	1
4	Carol	2024-01-01	Present	Bob	1
5	Alice	2024-01-02	Present		
6	Bob	2024-01-02	Present		
7	Carol	2024-01-02	Absent		

Objective: Write a function to summarize monthly attendance for a team, counting days present.

Sample Data:

Employee	Date	Status
Alice	2024-01-01	Present
Bob	2024-01-01	Absent
Carol	2024-01-01	Present
Alice	2024-01-02	Present
Bob	2024-01-02	Present
Carol	2024-01-02	Absent

Learning Outcomes:
- Learn to group and count data based on multiple criteria (employee and date).

- Practice aggregating data to provide a monthly summary of attendance.

Code Example:

```
/**
 * Summarizes monthly attendance for a team.
 *
 * @param {range} employees The range containing employee
names.
 * @param {range} dates The range containing dates.
 * @param {range} statuses The range containing attendance
statuses.
 * @return {array | string} An array listing each employee and
their total days present for the month, or an error message if
input data is invalid.
 * @customfunction
 */
function
MONTHLY_ATTENDANCE_SUMMARY(employees, dates,
statuses) {
const attendance = {};
for (let i = 0; i < employees.length; i++) {
const employee = employees[i][0];
const status = statuses[i][0];
if (typeof employee === 'string' && status === 'Present') {
attendance[employee] = (attendance[employee] || 0) + 1;
}
}
const result = Object.entries(attendance).map(([employee,
daysPresent]) => [employee, daysPresent]);
return result.length > 0 ? result : "No valid attendance data!";
}
```

Steps:

1. Paste the code into a new Apps Script project.
2. Save the changes and return to Google Sheets.
3. Enter the sample data into columns A1:C7.

4. Use the function like
    =MONTHLY_ATTENDANCE_SUMMARY(A2:A7,
    B2:B7, C2:C7).

Expected Result: The function will return an array listing each employee and the number of days they were present in the month.

Determine Employee Satisfaction Rating

C2	▾	fx =AVERAGE_SATISFACTION_RATING(A2:A8, B2:B8)	
	A	B	C
1	Employee	Satisfaction Rating	
2	Alice	4	4.00
3	Bob	3	
4	Carol	5	
5	David	4	
6	Emily	3	
7	Frank	4	
8	George	5	

Objective: Write a function to calculate the average satisfaction rating for employees based on survey responses.
Sample Data:

Employee	Satisfaction Rating
Alice	4
Bob	3
Carol	5
David	4
Emily	3
Frank	4
George	5

Learning Outcomes:
- Learn to calculate average values from a dataset.

- Practice handling numerical data and understanding employee satisfaction trends.

Code Example:

```
/**
 * Calculates the average satisfaction rating for employees.
 *
 * @param {range} employees The range containing employee names.
 * @param {range} ratings The range containing satisfaction ratings.
 * @return {number|string} The average satisfaction rating or an error message if input data is invalid.
 * @customfunction
 */
function AVERAGE_SATISFACTION_RATING(employees, ratings) {
let totalRating = 0;
let count = 0;
for (let i = 0; i < ratings.length; i++) {
const rating = ratings[i][0];
if (typeof rating === 'number') {
totalRating += rating;
count++;
}
}
if (count > 0) {
return (totalRating / count).toFixed(2);
} else {
return "Invalid or empty data!";
}
}
```

Steps:

1. Paste the code into a new Apps Script project.
2. Save the changes and return to Google Sheets.
3. Enter the sample data into columns A1:B8.

4. Use the function like
   =AVERAGE_SATISFACTION_RATING(A2:A8, B2:B8).

Expected Result: The function will return the average satisfaction rating based on the provided data.

Check Inventory for Expired Products

C2	▾	fx =CHECK_EXPIRED_PRODUCTS(A2:A6, B2:B6)		
	A	B	**C**	D
1	Product	Expiration Date		
2	Milk	2024-05-01	Milk	
3	Cheese	2024-06-15	Butter	
4	Butter	2024-04-20	Yogurt	
5	Yogurt	2024-05-10	Eggs	
6	Eggs	2024-05-25		

Objective: Write a function to identify expired products based on their expiration dates.

Sample Data:

Learning Outcomes:

- Learn to compare dates to determine product expiry.
- Practice filtering data based on a condition (expiration date before today).

Code Example:

```
/**
* Identifies expired products based on their expiration dates.
*
* @param {range} products The range containing product names.
* @param {range} expirationDates The range containing expiration dates.
* @return {array | string} An array listing expired products, or an error message if no expired products are found.
* @customfunction
*/
function CHECK_EXPIRED_PRODUCTS(products, expirationDates) {
```

```
const today = new Date();
const result = [];
for (let i = 0; i < products.length; i++) {
  const product = products[i][0];
  const expirationDate = new Date(expirationDates[i][0]);
  if (!isNaN(expirationDate) && expirationDate < today) {
    result.push([product]);
  }
}
return result.length > 0 ? result : "No expired products found.";
}
```

Steps:

1. Paste the code into a new Apps Script project.
2. Save the changes and return to Google Sheets.
3. Enter the sample data into columns A1:B6.
4. Use the function like
   =CHECK_EXPIRED_PRODUCTS(A2:A6, B2:B6).

Expected Result: The function will return an array listing any products that have expired.

Compute Total Sales and Average per Salesperson

C2	▾	fx =TOTAL_AND_AVERAGE_SALES(A2:A8, B2:B8)		
	A	B	C	D	E
1	Salesperson	Sale Amount			
2	Alice	150	Alice	650	216.67
3	Bob	300	Bob	750	375.00
4	Alice	200	Carol	650	325.00
5	Carol	250			
6	Bob	450			
7	Alice	300			
8	Carol	400			

Objective: Write a function to compute total sales and average sales per transaction for each salesperson.

Sample Data:

Salesperson	Sale Amount

Alice	150
Bob	300
Alice	200
Carol	250
Bob	450
Alice	300
Carol	400

Learning Outcomes:
- Practice aggregating and averaging data based on groups (by salesperson).
- Learn to output multiple types of calculated data (total and average).

Code Example:

```
/**
 * Computes total sales and average sales per transaction for
each salesperson.
 *
 * @param {range} salespeople The range containing
salesperson names.
 * @param {range} amounts The range containing sale
amounts.
 * @return {array | string} An array listing each salesperson
with total and average sales, or an error message if input data
is invalid.
 * @customfunction
 */
function TOTAL_AND_AVERAGE_SALES(salespeople,
amounts) {
 const salesData = {};
 for (let i = 0; i < salespeople.length; i++) {
 const salesperson = salespeople[i][0];
 const amount = amounts[i][0];
 if (!salesData[salesperson]) {
```

```javascript
  salesData[salesperson] = { total: 0, transactions: 0 };
}
salesData[salesperson].total += amount;
salesData[salesperson].transactions++;
}
const result = Object.entries(salesData).map(([salesperson,
data]) => [
 salesperson, data.total, (data.total /
data.transactions).toFixed(2)
]);
return result.length > 0 ? result : "No valid sales data!";
}
```

Steps:

1. Paste the code into a new Apps Script project.
2. Save the changes and return to Google Sheets.
3. Enter the sample data into columns A1:B8.
4. Use the function like
   =TOTAL_AND_AVERAGE_SALES(A2:A8, B2:B8).

Expected Result: The function will return an array listing each salesperson along with their total sales and average sales per transaction.

Calculate Daily Average Sales

C2	▾	f_x =DAILY_AVERAGE_SALES(A2:A8, B2:B8)		
	A	B	C	D
1	Day	Sales		
2	Monday	500	550.00	
3	Tuesday	600		
4	Wednesday	550		
5	Thursday	650		
6	Friday	700		
7	Saturday	400		
8	Sunday	450		

Objective: Develop a function to calculate the daily average sales from a week's worth of sales data.

Sample Data:

Day	Sales
Monday	500
Tuesday	600
Wednesday	550
Thursday	650
Friday	700
Saturday	400
Sunday	450

Learning Outcomes:
- Learn to aggregate sales data and calculate averages.
- Practice applying basic arithmetic functions to real-world business metrics.

Code Example:

```
/**
 * Calculates the daily average sales from a week's data.
 *
 * @param {range} days The range containing day names.
 * @param {range} sales The range containing sales data for
each day.
 * @return {number | string} The daily average sales or an
error message if input data is invalid.
 * @customfunction
 */
function DAILY_AVERAGE_SALES(days, sales) {
const totalSales = sales.reduce((acc, val) => acc + val[0], 0);
const daysCount = sales.length;
if (daysCount > 0) {
return (totalSales / daysCount).toFixed(2);
} else {
return "Invalid or empty data!";
}
}
```

Steps:

1. Paste the code into a new Apps Script project.
2. Save the changes and return to Google Sheets.
3. Enter the sample data into columns A1:B8.
4. Use the function like =DAILY_AVERAGE_SALES(A2:A8, B2:B8).

Expected Result: The function will return the average daily sales, calculated from the given week's data.

Identify Products with Price Changes

D2	▾	ƒx =IDENTIFY_PRICE_CHANGES(A2:A6, B2:B6, C2:C6)			
	A	B	C	D	E	F
1	Product	Price Period 1	Price Period 2			
2	Pen	1.5	1.75	Pen	1.5	1.75
3	Notebook	2	2	Eraser	0.5	0.45
4	Eraser	0.5	0.45	Marker	1.2	1.25
5	Marker	1.2	1.25	Backpack	22	20
6	Backpack	22	20			

Objective: Create a function to detect products that have experienced a change in price between two time periods.

Sample Data:

Product	Price Period 1	Price Period 2
Pen	1.5	1.75
Notebook	2	2
Eraser	0.5	0.45
Marker	1.2	1.25
Backpack	22	20

Learning Outcomes:
- Learn to compare data across different periods.
- Practice filtering data based on conditional logic to identify changes.

Code Example:
```
/**
 * Identifies products that have changed in price between two
periods.
```

```
*
* @param {range} products The range containing product
names.
* @param {range} prices1 The range containing prices in
period 1.
* @param {range} prices2 The range containing prices in
period 2.
* @return {array | string} An array listing products with price
changes, or an error message if no changes are found.
* @customfunction
*/
function IDENTIFY_PRICE_CHANGES(products, prices1,
prices2) {
const result = [];
for (let i = 0; i < products.length; i++) {
const product = products[i][0];
const price1 = prices1[i][0];
const price2 = prices2[i][0];
if (price1 !== price2) {
result.push([product, price1, price2]);
}
}
return result.length > 0 ? result : "No price changes
detected.";
}
```

Steps:
1. Paste the code into a new Apps Script project.
2. Save the changes and return to Google Sheets.
3. Enter the sample data into columns A1:C6.
4. Use the function like
   =IDENTIFY_PRICE_CHANGES(A2:A6, B2:B6,
   C2:C6).

Expected Result: The function will return an array of products whose prices have changed, listing the old and new prices.

Summarize Customer Feedback by Rating

	A	B	C	D
1	Customer	Rating		
2	Alice	5	1	1
3	Bob	4	2	1
4	Carol	5	3	1
5	David	3	4	1
6	Emily	2	5	3
7	Frank	1		
8	George	5		

Objective: Write a function to count the number of feedback entries per rating scale (1-5).

Sample Data:

Customer	Rating
Alice	5
Bob	4
Carol	5
David	3
Emily	2
Frank	1
George	5

Learning Outcomes:
- Learn to categorize and count data based on specific criteria.
- Practice using arrays and mapping techniques to summarize data efficiently.

Code Example:

```
/**
 * Summarizes customer feedback by rating scale.
 *
 * @param {range} customers The range containing customer
 names.
```

* @param {range} ratings The range containing customer ratings.
 * @return {array | string} An array summarizing the count of ratings, or an error message if input data is invalid.
 * @customfunction
 */

```
function SUMMARIZE_FEEDBACK_BY_RATING(customers, ratings) {
const ratingCounts = {1: 0, 2: 0, 3: 0, 4: 0, 5: 0};
for (let i = 0; i < ratings.length; i++) {
const rating = ratings[i][0];
if (ratingCounts.hasOwnProperty(rating)) {
ratingCounts[rating]++;
}
}
const result = Object.keys(ratingCounts).map(key => [key, ratingCounts[key]]);
return result.length > 0 ? result : "No feedback data found.";
}
```

Steps:
1. Paste the code into a new Apps Script project.
2. Save the changes and return to Google Sheets.
3. Enter the sample data into columns A1:B8.
4. Use the function like =SUMMARIZE_FEEDBACK_BY_RATING(A2:A8, B2:B8).

Expected Result: The function will return a summary of how many feedback entries exist for each rating from 1 to 5.

Calculate Total Discounts Given

D2	▼	_fx_ =TOTAL_DISCOUNTS_GIVEN(A2:A6, B2:B6, C2:C6)		

	A	B	C	D
1	Product	Original Price	Discounted Price	
2	T-shirt	20	15	45
3	Jeans	50	45	
4	Sweater	60	50	
5	Jacket	100	80	
6	Hat	25	20	

Objective: Write a function to calculate the total amount of discounts given based on the original prices and discounted prices.

Sample Data:

Product	Original Price	Discounted Price
T-shirt	20	15
Jeans	50	45
Sweater	60	50
Jacket	100	80
Hat	25	20

Learning Outcomes:
- Learn to calculate the difference between original and discounted prices.
- Understand how to aggregate savings across multiple items.

Code Example:

```
/**
 * Calculates the total discounts given.
 *
 * @param {range} products The range containing product names.
 * @param {range} originalPrices The range containing original prices.
```

```
 * @param {range} discountedPrices The range containing
discounted prices.
 * @return {number|string} The total amount of discounts
given or an error message if input data is invalid.
 * @customfunction
 */
function TOTAL_DISCOUNTS_GIVEN(products,
originalPrices, discountedPrices) {
let totalDiscount = 0;
for (let i = 0; i < products.length; i++) {
const originalPrice = originalPrices[i][0];
const discountedPrice = discountedPrices[i][0];
if (typeof originalPrice === 'number' && typeof
discountedPrice === 'number') {
totalDiscount += originalPrice - discountedPrice;
}
}
return totalDiscount > 0 ? totalDiscount : "No discounts
given or invalid data.";
}
```

Steps:

1. Paste the code into a new Apps Script project.
2. Save the changes and return to Google Sheets.
3. Enter the sample data into columns A1:C6.
4. Use the function like
   =TOTAL_DISCOUNTS_GIVEN(A2:A6, B2:B6, C2:C6).

Expected Result: The function will return the total amount of discounts given across all products.

Monitor Project Deadline Compliance

C2	▾	ƒx =MONITOR_PROJECT_DEADLINES(A2:A6, B2:B6)		
	A	B	C	D
1	Project	Deadline		
2	Development	2024-04-15	Development	
3	Research	2024-05-01	Research	
4	Marketing	2024-04-22	Marketing	
5	Expansion	2024-05-05	Expansion	
6	Training	2024-04-28	Training	

Objective: Develop a function to monitor and report projects that are overdue based on their deadlines.

Sample Data:

Project	Deadline
Development	2024-04-15
Research	2024-05-01
Marketing	2024-04-22
Expansion	2024-05-05
Training	2024-04-28

Learning Outcomes:
- Practice working with date comparisons.
- Learn to identify overdue tasks relative to the current date.

Code Example:

```
/**
 * Monitors and reports projects that are overdue.
 *
 * @param {range} projects The range containing project names.
 * @param {range} deadlines The range containing project deadlines.
 * @return {array | string} An array listing overdue projects or an error message if no projects are overdue.
 * @customfunction
```

```
*/
function MONITOR_PROJECT_DEADLINES(projects,
deadlines) {
const today = new Date();
const result = [];
for (let i = 0; i < projects.length; i++) {
const project = projects[i][0];
const deadline = new Date(deadlines[i][0]);
if (deadline < today) {
result.push([project]);
}
}
return result.length > 0 ? result : "No projects are overdue.";
}
```

Steps:
1. Paste the code into a new Apps Script project.
2. Save the changes and return to Google Sheets.
3. Enter the sample data into columns A1:B6.
4. Use the function like
   =MONITOR_PROJECT_DEADLINES(A2:A6, B2:B6).

Expected Result: The function will return an array of projects that are overdue based on their set deadlines.

Classify Emails by Content Keywords

C2	▾	*fx* =CLASSIFY_EMAILS_BY_CONTENT(A2:A6, B2:B6)		
	A	B	C	D
1	Email	Content		
2	Email 1	"I have a question regarding my order."	Email 1	Inquiry
3	Email 2	"Thank you for the excellent service!"	Email 2	Praise
4	Email 3	"I am unhappy with the product quality."	Email 3	Complaint
5	Email 4	"Can you help me with my account?"	Email 4	Inquiry
6	Email 5	"Great job on the recent project!"	Email 5	Praise

Objective: Write a function to classify emails based on content keywords into categories such as 'Inquiry', 'Complaint', 'Praise'.

Sample Data:

Email	Content

Email 1	"I have a question regarding my order."
Email 2	"Thank you for the excellent service!"
Email 3	"I am unhappy with the product quality."
Email 4	"Can you help me with my account?"
Email 5	"Great job on the recent project!"

Learning Outcomes:
- Learn to apply simple text analysis for categorization.
- Practice using string methods to identify content types.

Code Example:
```
/**
 * Classifies emails based on content keywords.
 *
 * @param {range} emails The range containing email
identifiers.
 * @param {range} contents The range containing email
contents.
 * @return {array | string} An array listing emails with their
categories, or an error message if classification fails.
 * @customfunction
 */
function CLASSIFY_EMAILS_BY_CONTENT(emails,
contents) {
 const categories = [];
for (let i = 0; i < emails.length; i++) {
 const email = emails[i][0];
 const content = contents[i][0].toLowerCase();
 if (content.includes("thank you") || content.includes("great
job")) {
 categories.push([email, "Praise"]);
 } else if (content.includes("unhappy") ||
content.includes("complaint")) {
 categories.push([email, "Complaint"]);
```

```
} else if (content.includes("question") ||
content.includes("help")) {
categories.push([email, "Inquiry"]);
} else {
categories.push([email, "Other"]);
}
}
return categories.length > 0 ? categories : "Unable to classify
emails.";
}
```

Steps:
1. Paste the code into a new Apps Script project.
2. Save the changes and return to Google Sheets.
3. Enter the sample data into columns A1:B6.
4. Use the function like
   =CLASSIFY_EMAILS_BY_CONTENT(A2:A6, B2:B6).

Expected Result: The function will classify each email into a category based on its content keywords, helping organize responses or follow-up actions.

Compute Total Cost by Order Quantity

D2	▾	*fx* =TOTAL_COST_BY_ORDER_QUANTITY(A2:A6, B2:B6, C2:C6)		
	A	B	C	D	E
1	Product	Quantity	Unit Price		
2	Notebook	50	3	Notebook	150.00
3	Pen	100	1.5	Pen	150.00
4	Binder	30	4.5	Binder	135.00
5	Stapler	20	8	Stapler	160.00
6	Calculator	15	12	Calculator	180.00

Objective: Create a function to compute the total cost for each product based on its order quantity and unit price.

Sample Data:

Product	Quantity	Unit Price
Notebook	50	3
Pen	100	1.5

Binder	30	4.5
Stapler	20	8
Calculator	15	12

Learning Outcomes:
- Learn to multiply quantities by unit prices to compute total costs.
- Practice using arrays and arithmetic operations to process financial data.

Code Example:

```
/**
 * Computes the total cost for each product based on quantity
and unit price.
 *
 * @param {range} products The range containing product
names.
 * @param {range} quantities The range containing quantities
ordered.
 * @param {range} unitPrices The range containing unit prices
of products.
 * @return {array | string} An array listing products and their
total costs, or an error message if input data is invalid.
 * @customfunction
 */
function TOTAL_COST_BY_ORDER_QUANTITY(products,
quantities, unitPrices) {
 const result = [];
for (let i = 0; i < products.length; i++) {
 const product = products[i][0];
 const quantity = quantities[i][0];
 const unitPrice = unitPrices[i][0];
 if (typeof quantity === 'number' && typeof unitPrice ===
'number') {
 const totalCost = quantity * unitPrice;
 result.push([product, totalCost.toFixed(2)]);
 }
```

```
}
  return result.length > 0 ? result : "Invalid or empty data!";
}
```

Steps:

1. Paste the code into a new Apps Script project.
2. Save the changes and return to Google Sheets.
3. Enter the sample data into columns A1:C6.
4. Use the function like
   =TOTAL_COST_BY_ORDER_QUANTITY(A2:A6, B2:B6, C2:C6).

Expected Result: The function will return an array listing each product and its total cost based on the order quantity and unit price.

10 - Sheets Coding Examples dates and summaries

Common sheets functions that can be used to calculate and output results from data provided.

Count Customer Visits by Month

C2		▼	*fx* =VISITS_BY_MONTH(A2:A8, B2:B8)		
	A	**B**	**C**	**D**	
1	Customer	Visit Date			
2	Alice	2024-01-05	Alice - 2024-01	2	
3	Bob	2024-01-10	Bob - 2024-01	1	
4	Alice	2024-01-20	Carol - 2024-01	1	
5	Carol	2024-01-15	Alice - 2024-02	1	
6	Alice	2024-02-01	Bob - 2024-02	1	
7	Bob	2024-02-05	Carol - 2024-02	1	
8	Carol	2024-02-15			

Objective: Develop a function to count the number of visits each customer made in a given month.

Sample Data:

Customer	Visit Date
Alice	2024-01-05
Bob	2024-01-10
Alice	2024-01-20
Carol	2024-01-15
Alice	2024-02-01
Bob	2024-02-05
Carol	2024-02-15

Learning Outcomes:
- Practice extracting the month from date data and grouping counts by month.

- Learn to handle date data and use conditional counting.

Code Example:

```
/**
* Counts the number of visits each customer made per month.
*
* @param {range} customers The range containing customer names.
* @param {range} visitDates The range containing dates of visits.
* @return {array | string} An array listing each customer with their visit counts by month, or an error message if input data is invalid.
* @customfunction
*/
function VISITS_BY_MONTH(customers, visitDates) {
 const visits = {};
for (let i = 0; i < customers.length; i++) {
 const customer = customers[i][0];
 const visitDate = new Date(visitDates[i][0]);
 const month = visitDate.getMonth() + 1; // Get the month
(0-based index, hence +1)
 const year = visitDate.getFullYear();
 const key = customer + ' - ' + year + '-' + (month < 10 ? '0' +
month : month);
 if (!visits[key]) visits[key] = 0;
 visits[key]++;
}
 const result = Object.entries(visits).map(([key, count]) =>
[key, count]);
 return result.length > 0 ? result : "No visits recorded.";
}
```

Steps:

1. Paste the code into a new Apps Script project.
2. Save the changes and return to Google Sheets.
3. Enter the sample data into columns A1:B8.

4. Use the function like =VISITS_BY_MONTH(A2:A8, B2:B8).

Expected Result: The function will return an array listing each customer along with their visit counts organized by month and year.

Identify Out-of-Stock Products

C2	▼	fx =IDENTIFY_OUT_OF_STOCK_PRODUCTS(A2:A6, B2:B6)		
	A	B	C	D
1	Product	Stock Quantity		
2	Notebook	20	Pen	
3	Pen	0	Stapler	
4	Binder	50		
5	Stapler	0		
6	Calculator	15		

Objective: Write a function to identify products that are out of stock.

Sample Data:

Product	Stock Quantity
Notebook	20
Pen	0
Binder	50
Stapler	0
Calculator	15

Learning Outcomes:
- Learn to filter and identify products based on a specific stock condition.
- Practice using conditional statements to create specific outputs.

Code Example:
```
/**
 * Identifies products that are out of stock.
 *
```

* @param {range} products The range containing product
names.
 * @param {range} stockQuantities The range containing stock
quantities.
 * @return {array | string} An array listing out-of-stock
products, or an error message if all products are in stock.
 * @customfunction
 */
function
IDENTIFY_OUT_OF_STOCK_PRODUCTS(products,
stockQuantities) {
 const result = [];
for (let i = 0; i < products.length; i++) {
 const product = products[i][0];
 const stock = stockQuantities[i][0];
 if (stock === 0) {
 result.push([product]);
 }
 }
 return result.length > 0 ? result : "All products are in stock.";
}

Steps:
1. Paste the code into a new Apps Script project.
2. Save the changes and return to Google Sheets.
3. Enter the sample data into columns A1:B6.
4. Use the function like
   =IDENTIFY_OUT_OF_STOCK_PRODUCTS(A2:A6,
   B2:B6).

Expected Result: The function will return an array listing
products that are out of stock.

Calculate Employee Bonus Based on Performance

Objective: Write a function to calculate an employee's annual bonus based on their performance rating. The bonus is calculated as a percentage of their annual salary, where a rating of 1 gives no bonus, and each additional rating point increases the bonus by 5%.

Sample Data:

Employee	Annual Salary	Performance Rating
Alice	50000	3
Bob	60000	4
Carol	55000	2
David	48000	5
Emily	75000	1

Learning Outcomes:
- Learn to apply a formula based on conditional data inputs.
- Practice simple mathematical calculations to derive bonus amounts.

Code Example:

```
/**
 * Calculates the annual bonus based on performance ratings.
 *
 * @param {range} employees The range containing employee names.
 * @param {range} salaries The range containing annual salaries.
```

* @param {range} ratings The range containing performance ratings.
 * @return {array | string} An array listing employees, their performance ratings, and their bonus, or an error message if input data is invalid.
 * @customfunction
 */

```
function CALCULATE_BONUS(employees, salaries, ratings) {
const results = [];
for (let i = 0; i < employees.length; i++) {
const employee = employees[i][0];
const salary = salaries[i][0];
const rating = ratings[i][0];
if (typeof salary === 'number' && typeof rating === 'number' && rating >= 1 && rating <= 5) {
const bonusPercentage = (rating - 1) * 5;
const bonus = salary * (bonusPercentage / 100);
results.push([employee, rating, bonus.toFixed(2)]);
} else {
results.push([employee, rating, "Invalid data"]);
}
}
return results.length > 0 ? results : "No valid data!";
}
```

Steps:
1. Paste the code into a new Apps Script project.
2. Save the changes and return to Google Sheets.
3. Enter the sample data into columns A1:C6.
4. Use the function like =CALCULATE_BONUS(A2:A6, B2:B6, C2:C6).

Expected Result: The function will calculate and return the annual bonuses based on performance ratings, alongside the employee name and their rating.

Summarize Monthly Expenses by Category

D2   ▼   _fx_ =SUMMARIZE_MONTHLY_EXPENSES(A2:A7, B2:B7, C2:C7)

	A	B	C	D	E	F
1	Month	Category	Expense			
2	January	Utilities	200	January	Utilities	200
3	January	Groceries	450	January	Groceries	450
4	February	Utilities	180	February	Utilities	180
5	February	Groceries	400	February	Groceries	400
6	March	Utilities	210	March	Utilities	210
7	March	Groceries	460	March	Groceries	460

Objective: Develop a function to summarize expenses by category for each month.

Sample Data:

Month	Category	Expense
January	Utilities	200
January	Groceries	450
February	Utilities	180
February	Groceries	400
March	Utilities	210
March	Groceries	460

Learning Outcomes:
- Learn to group and sum data based on multiple criteria.
- Practice extracting and presenting aggregated financial data.

Code Example:
```
/**
 * Summarizes monthly expenses by category.
 *
 * @param {range} months The range containing month names.
 * @param {range} categories The range containing expense categories.
 * @param {range} expenses The range containing expense amounts.
```

```
* @return {array | string} An array listing each month with
expenses summarized by category, or an error message if
input data is invalid.
* @customfunction
*/
function SUMMARIZE_MONTHLY_EXPENSES(months,
categories, expenses) {
 const monthlySummary = {};
for (let i = 0; i < months.length; i++) {
 const month = months[i][0];
 const category = categories[i][0];
 const expense = expenses[i][0];
 if (!monthlySummary[month]) monthlySummary[month] =
{};
 if (!monthlySummary[month][category])
monthlySummary[month][category] = 0;
 monthlySummary[month][category] += expense;
 }
 const results = [];
Object.keys(monthlySummary).forEach(month => {
Object.keys(monthlySummary[month]).forEach(category =>
{
 results.push([month, category,
monthlySummary[month][category]]);
 });
 });
 return results.length > 0 ? results : "No valid data!";
}
```

Steps:

1. Paste the code into a new Apps Script project.
2. Save the changes and return to Google Sheets.
3. Enter the sample data into columns A1:C7.
4. Use the function like
    =SUMMARIZE_MONTHLY_EXPENSES(A2:A7,
    B2:B7, C2:C7).

Expected Result: The function will return a summary of expenses by category for each month, detailing the total spent in each category.

Evaluate Product Inventory Needs

	A	B	C	D
1	Product	Current Stock	Minimum Stock	
2	Notebook	25	30	Notebook
3	Pen	150	100	Binder
4	Binder	15	20	Calculator
5	Stapler	10	10	
6	Calculator	5	7	

Objective: Write a function to evaluate which products need to be reordered based on their current stock and a predefined minimum stock level.

Sample Data:

Product	Current Stock	Minimum Stock
Notebook	25	30
Pen	150	100
Binder	15	20
Stapler	10	10
Calculator	5	7

Learning Outcomes:
- Practice using conditional checks to identify inventory needs.
- Learn to compare current inventory levels against minimum requirements.

Code Example:
```
/**
 * Evaluates which products need to be reordered.
 *
```

* @param {range} products The range containing product names.
 * @param {range} currentStocks The range containing current stock quantities.
 * @param {range} minimumStocks The range containing minimum stock levels.
 * @return {array | string} An array listing products that need reordering, or an error message if no reordering is needed.
 * @customfunction
 */

```
function EVALUATE_INVENTORY_NEEDS(products,
currentStocks, minimumStocks) {
 const results = [];
for (let i = 0; i < products.length; i++) {
 const product = products[i][0];
 const currentStock = currentStocks[i][0];
 const minimumStock = minimumStocks[i][0];
 if (currentStock < minimumStock) {
 results.push([product]);
 }
 }
 return results.length > 0 ? results : "All products are
sufficiently stocked.";
 }
```

Steps:
1. Paste the code into a new Apps Script project.
2. Save the changes and return to Google Sheets.
3. Enter the sample data into columns A1:C6.
4. Use the function like =EVALUATE_INVENTORY_NEEDS(A2:A6, B2:B6, C2:C6).

Expected Result: The function will return a list of products that need reordering based on their current stock levels being below the minimum required.

Calculate Customer Lifetime Value (CLV)

	A	B	C	D		E	F
1	Customer	Annual Spending	Retention Rate	Discount Rate			
2	Alice	1200	0.8	0.1		Alice	3200.00
3	Bob	1500	0.7	0.1		Bob	2625.00
4	Carol	1800	0.5	0.1		Carol	1500.00
5	David	1000	0.9	0.1		David	4500.00
6	Emily	1600	0.4	0.1		Emily	914.29

Objective: Develop a function to calculate the Customer Lifetime Value based on annual spending, retention rate, and discount rate.

Sample Data:

Customer	Annual Spending	Retention Rate	Discount Rate
Alice	1200	0.8	0.1
Bob	1500	0.7	0.1
Carol	1800	0.5	0.1
David	1000	0.9	0.1
Emily	1600	0.4	0.1

Learning Outcomes:
- Learn to apply the formula for calculating CLV:
- CLV=Annual Spending×Retention RateDiscount Rate+(1−Retention Rate)
- CLV=
  - Discount Rate+(1−Retention Rate)
  - Annual Spending×Retention Rate
    -
- .
- Practice handling complex mathematical operations and understanding customer behavior metrics.

Code Example:
```
/**
* Calculates Customer Lifetime Value.
*
```

```
 * @param {range} customers The range containing customer
names.
 * @param {range} annualSpendings The range containing
annual spending amounts.
 * @param {range} retentionRates The range containing
customer retention rates.
 * @param {range} discountRates The range containing the
discount rates.
 * @return {array | string} An array listing customers with
their CLV, or an error message if input data is invalid.
 * @customfunction
 */
function CALCULATE_CLV(customers, annualSpendings,
retentionRates, discountRates) {
 const results = [];
for (let i = 0; i < customers.length; i++) {
 const customer = customers[i][0];
 const annualSpending = annualSpendings[i][0];
 const retentionRate = retentionRates[i][0];
 const discountRate = discountRates[i][0];
 if (typeof annualSpending === 'number' && typeof
retentionRate === 'number' && typeof discountRate ===
'number') {
 const clv = (annualSpending * retentionRate) / (discountRate
+ (1 - retentionRate));
 results.push([customer, clv.toFixed(2)]);
 }
 }
 return results.length > 0 ? results : "Invalid or empty data!";
}
```

Steps:

1. Paste the code into a new Apps Script project.
2. Save the changes and return to Google Sheets.
3. Enter the sample data into columns A1:D6.
4. Use the function like =CALCULATE_CLV(A2:A6,
    B2:B6, C2:C6, D2:D6).

Expected Result: The function will calculate and return each customer's lifetime value based on their spending habits and retention rates.

Summarize Product Reviews by Rating

C2	▾	ƒx =SUMMARIZE_REVIEWS_BY_RATING(A2:A7, B2:B7)			

	A	B	C	D	E
1	Product	Star Rating			
2	Product A	5	Product A	3	1
3	Product B	4	Product A	5	1
4	Product A	3	Product B	2	1
5	Product C	5	Product B	4	1
6	Product B	2	Product C	1	1
7	Product C	1	Product C	5	1

Objective: Write a function to count the number of product reviews at each star rating level.

Sample Data:

Product	Star Rating
Product A	5
Product B	4
Product A	3
Product C	5
Product B	2
Product C	1

Learning Outcomes:
- Learn to group and count occurrences based on multiple data points.
- Practice data aggregation and summarization skills.

Code Example:
```
/**
* Summarizes product reviews by star rating.
*
```

```
 * @param {range} products The range containing product
names.
 * @param {range} ratings The range containing star ratings.
 * @return {array | string} An array summarizing the number
of reviews per star rating for each product, or an error
message if input data is invalid.
 * @customfunction
 */
function SUMMARIZE_REVIEWS_BY_RATING(products,
ratings) {
 const summary = {};
 for (let i = 0; i < products.length; i++) {
 const product = products[i][0];
 const rating = ratings[i][0];
 if (!summary[product]) summary[product] = {1:0, 2:0, 3:0, 4:0,
5:0}; // Initialize if not exists
 if (summary[product][rating] !== undefined) {
 summary[product][rating]++;
 }
 }
 const results = [];
 Object.keys(summary).forEach(product => {
 Object.keys(summary[product]).forEach(rate => {
 if (summary[product][rate] > 0) { // Only include if there are
reviews
 results.push([product, rate, summary[product][rate]]);
 }
 });
 });
 return results.length > 0 ? results : "No review data found.";
}
```

Steps:

1. Paste the code into a new Apps Script project.
2. Save the changes and return to Google Sheets.
3. Enter the sample data into columns A1:B7.

4. Use the function like
   =SUMMARIZE_REVIEWS_BY_RATING(A2:A7, B2:B7).

Expected Result: The function will return a summary of product reviews, counting the number of times each star rating was given to each product.

Analyze Monthly Attendance Rates

D2   ▾   *fx* =ANALYZE_ATTENDANCE_RATES(A2:A6, B2:B6, C2:C6)

	A	B	C	D	E
1	Month	Attendance Count	Total Students		
2	January	18	20	March	70.00%
3	February	15	20		
4	March	14	20		
5	April	19	20		
6	May	15	20		

Objective: Develop a function to analyze the monthly attendance rate for a class, identifying months with attendance below 75%.

Sample Data:

Month	Attendance Count	Total Students
January	18	20
February	15	20
March	14	20
April	19	20
May	15	20

Learning Outcomes:
- Learn to calculate percentages and identify specific criteria.
- Practice using conditional statements to analyze attendance data.

Code Example:

```
/**
 * Analyzes monthly attendance rates to identify months with
 * attendance below 75%.
 *
 * @param {range} months The range containing month
 * names.
 * @param {range} attendanceCounts The range containing
 * attendance counts.
 * @param {range} totalStudents The range containing total
 * number of students.
 * @return {array | string} An array listing months with low
 * attendance rates, or an error message if all months meet the
 * threshold.
 * @customfunction
 */
function ANALYZE_ATTENDANCE_RATES(months,
attendanceCounts, totalStudents) {
const results = [];
for (let i = 0; i < months.length; i++) {
const month = months[i][0];
const attendanceCount = attendanceCounts[i][0];
const total = totalStudents[i][0];
const rate = (attendanceCount / total) * 100;
if (rate < 75) {
results.push([month, rate.toFixed(2) + "%"]);
}
}
return results.length > 0 ? results : "All months have
satisfactory attendance rates.";
}
```

Steps:

1. Paste the code into a new Apps Script project.
2. Save the changes and return to Google Sheets.
3. Enter the sample data into columns A1:C6.
4. Use the function like
   =ANALYZE_ATTENDANCE_RATES(A2:A6, B2:B6,
   C2:C6).

Expected Result: The function will return the months where the attendance rate was below 75%, highlighting potential issues with student engagement or attendance policies.

Calculate Total Event Duration

C2	▾	fx =TOTAL_EVENT_DURATION(A2:A6, B2:B6)

	A	B	C
1	Session	Duration (hours)	
2	Opening	2	9
3	Workshop 1	3	
4	Break	0.5	
5	Workshop 2	2.5	
6	Closing	1	

Objective: Write a function to calculate the total duration of an event across multiple sessions in hours.

Sample Data:

Session	Duration (hours)
Opening	2
Workshop 1	3
Break	0.5
Workshop 2	2.5
Closing	1

Learning Outcomes:
- Learn to aggregate data to compute total durations.
- Practice handling numerical data for sum calculations.

Code Example:

```
/**
* Calculates the total duration of an event from its sessions.
*
* @param {range} sessions The range containing session
names.
```

* @param {range} durations The range containing durations in hours for each session.
* @return {number | string} The total event duration in hours, or an error message if input data is invalid.
* @customfunction
*/

```
function TOTAL_EVENT_DURATION(sessions, durations) {
let totalDuration = 0;
for (let i = 0; i < durations.length; i++) {
const duration = durations[i][0];
if (typeof duration === 'number') {
totalDuration += duration;
} else {
return "Invalid duration data!";
}
}
return totalDuration;
}
```

Steps:

1. Paste the code into a new Apps Script project.
2. Save the changes and return to Google Sheets.
3. Enter the sample data into columns A1:B6.
4. Use the function like
   =TOTAL_EVENT_DURATION(A2:A6, B2:B6).

Expected Result: The function will return the total duration of the event, calculated by summing up the hours from each session.

Identify High-Priority Emails

C2   ▼ | *fx* =IDENTIFY_HIGH_PRIORITY_EMAILS(A2:A6, B2:B6)

	A	B	C
1	Email ID	Content	
2	E001	"Please review the documents at your earliest"	E002
3	E002	"Need this done ASAP!"	E004
4	E003	"Schedule a meeting for next week"	
5	E004	"URGENT: Update the proposal before noon"	
6	E005	"Can this wait until tomorrow?"	

Objective: Develop a function to flag emails with high-priority keywords such as "urgent", "asap", or "immediate".

Sample Data:

Email ID	Content
E001	"Please review the documents at your earliest"
E002	"Need this done ASAP!"
E003	"Schedule a meeting for next week"
E004	"URGENT: Update the proposal before noon"
E005	"Can this wait until tomorrow?"

Learning Outcomes:
- Learn to filter data based on the presence of specific keywords.
- Practice string manipulation and conditional checks.

Code Example:

```
/**
 * Identifies high-priority emails based on content keywords.
 *
 * @param {range} emails The range containing email IDs.
 * @param {range} contents The range containing the content
of each email.
 * @return {array | string} An array listing high-priority email
IDs, or an error message if no high-priority emails are found.
 * @customfunction
 */
function IDENTIFY_HIGH_PRIORITY_EMAILS(emails,
contents) {
const highPriorityKeywords = ["urgent", "asap",
"immediate"];
const highPriorityEmails = [];
for (let i = 0; i < emails.length; i++) {
const content = contents[i][0].toLowerCase();
if (highPriorityKeywords.some(keyword =>
content.includes(keyword))) {
```

highPriorityEmails.push([emails[i][0]]);
}
}
return highPriorityEmails.length > 0 ? highPriorityEmails :
"No high-priority emails identified.";
}

Steps:

1. Paste the code into a new Apps Script project.
2. Save the changes and return to Google Sheets.
3. Enter the sample data into columns A1:B6.
4. Use the function like
   =IDENTIFY_HIGH_PRIORITY_EMAILS(A2:A6,
   B2:B6).

Expected Result: The function will identify and return a list of email IDs that contain high-priority keywords, indicating urgent attention is needed.

Calculate Average Product Rating

C2	▼	ƒx =AVERAGE_PRODUCT_RATING(A2:A7, B2:B7)	
	A	B	C	D
1	Product	Rating		
2	Laptop	5	Laptop	4.00
3	Laptop	4	Smartphone	4.67
4	Smartphone	5		
5	Laptop	3		
6	Smartphone	4		
7	Smartphone	5		

Objective: Write a function to calculate the average rating for products based on customer reviews.

Sample Data:

Product	Rating
Laptop	5
Laptop	4
Smartphone	5

Laptop	3
Smartphone	4
Smartphone	5

Learning Outcomes:
- Learn to group data by product and calculate average values.
- Practice using arrays and loops to manipulate and analyze data.

Code Example:

```
/**
 * Calculates the average rating for each product based on
customer reviews.
 *
 * @param {range} products The range containing product
names.
 * @param {range} ratings The range containing ratings.
 * @return {array | string} An array listing each product with
its average rating, or an error message if input data is invalid.
 * @customfunction
 */
function AVERAGE_PRODUCT_RATING(products, ratings)
{
const ratingSummary = {};
for (let i = 0; i < products.length; i++) {
const product = products[i][0];
const rating = ratings[i][0];
if (!ratingSummary[product]) {
ratingSummary[product] = { total: 0, count: 0 };
}
ratingSummary[product].total += rating;
ratingSummary[product].count++;
}
const results = [];
Object.keys(ratingSummary).forEach(product => {
```

```
const average = ratingSummary[product].total /
ratingSummary[product].count;
results.push([product, average.toFixed(2)]);
});
return results.length > 0 ? results : "No valid data!";
}
```

Steps:

1. Paste the code into a new Apps Script project.
2. Save the changes and return to Google Sheets.
3. Enter the sample data into columns A1:B7.
4. Use the function like
   =AVERAGE_PRODUCT_RATING(A2:A7, B2:B7).

Expected Result: The function will compute and return the average rating for each product based on the customer reviews provided.

Track Task Completion Status

	A	B	C	D	E	F
1	Task	Due Date	Is Completed			
2	Report	2024-05-10	TRUE	Report	5/10/2024	Completed
3	Presentation	2024-05-15	FALSE	Presentation	5/15/2024	Pending
4	Assignment	2024-05-20	TRUE	Assignment	5/20/2024	Completed
5	Review	2024-05-25	FALSE	Review	5/25/2024	Pending
6	Feedback	2024-05-30	TRUE	Feedback	5/30/2024	Completed

Objective: Write a function to track the completion status of tasks, marking them as "Completed" if finished or "Pending" if not.

Sample Data:

Task	Due Date	Is Completed
Report	2024-05-10	TRUE
Presentation	2024-05-15	FALSE
Assignment	2024-05-20	TRUE
Review	2024-05-25	FALSE
Feedback	2024-05-30	TRUE

Learning Outcomes:
- Learn to use conditional logic to determine task status.
- Practice creating user-friendly status outputs for task tracking.

Code Example:

```
/**
* Tracks the completion status of tasks.
*
* @param {range} tasks The range containing task names.
* @param {range} dueDates The range containing task due
dates.
* @param {range} completionStatus The range containing
boolean values indicating task completion.
* @return {array | string} An array listing tasks with their
status as "Completed" or "Pending", or an error message if
input data is invalid.
* @customfunction
*/
function TRACK_TASK_COMPLETION(tasks, dueDates,
completionStatus) {
const results = [];
for (let i = 0; i < tasks.length; i++) {
const task = tasks[i][0];
const isCompleted = completionStatus[i][0];
const status = isCompleted ? "Completed" : "Pending";
results.push([task, dueDates[i][0], status]);
}
return results.length > 0 ? results : "No tasks to display.";
}
```

Steps:
1. Paste the code into a new Apps Script project.
2. Save the changes and return to Google Sheets.
3. Enter the sample data into columns A1:C6.
4. Use the function like
   =TRACK_TASK_COMPLETION(A2:A6, B2:B6, C2:C6).

Expected Result: The function will list each task along with its due date and status, either "Completed" or "Pending".

11 : Projects and Calculating Outputs

The following exercises provide more examples of how to use a custom formula in Google Sheets using Apps Script to create customized output into multiple columns within a Spreadsheet.

Monitor Project Phase Timeliness

D2	▼	ƒx	=MONITOR_PROJECT_TIMELINESS(A2:A6, B2:B6, C2:C6)		
	A	B	C	D	E
1	Project	Phase End Date	Status		
2	Project 1	2024-05-10	In Progress	Project 1	Delayed
3	Project 2	2024-05-05	Completed	Project 2	Completed
4	Project 3	2024-05-15	In Progress	Project 3	Delayed
5	Project 4	2024-05-03	In Progress	Project 4	Delayed
6	Project 5	2024-05-02	Completed	Project 5	Completed

Objective: Create a function to monitor project phases, indicating if they are on schedule, delayed, or completed based on the current date and phase end dates.

Sample Data:

Project	Phase End Date	Status
Project 1	2024-05-10	In Progress
Project 2	2024-05-05	Completed
Project 3	2024-05-15	In Progress
Project 4	2024-05-03	In Progress
Project 5	2024-05-02	Completed

Learning Outcomes:
- Learn to compare dates to current date to evaluate timelines.

- Practice using date comparisons and logical operations to generate project status updates.

Code Example:

```
/**
* Monitors project phase timeliness, indicating if phases are
on schedule, delayed, or completed.
*
* @param {range} projects The range containing project
names.
* @param {range} phaseEndDates The range containing
phase end dates.
* @param {range} statuses The range containing current
status of each project.
* @return {array | string} An array listing each project with its
timeliness status, or an error message if data is invalid.
* @customfunction
*/
function MONITOR_PROJECT_TIMELINESS(projects,
phaseEndDates, statuses) {
const today = new Date();
const results = [];
for (let i = 0; i < projects.length; i++) {
const project = projects[i][0];
const endDate = new Date(phaseEndDates[i][0]);
const status = statuses[i][0];
const timeliness = status === "Completed" ? "Completed" :
(endDate < today ? "Delayed" : "On Schedule");
results.push([project, timeliness]);
}
return results.length > 0 ? results : "No projects to monitor.";
}
```

Steps:

1. Paste the code into a new Apps Script project.
2. Save the changes and return to Google Sheets.
3. Enter the sample data into columns A1:C6.

4. Use the function like
   =MONITOR_PROJECT_TIMELINESS(A2:A6, B2:B6, C2:C6).

Expected Result: The function will evaluate each project phase's timeliness, identifying whether they are on schedule, delayed, or already completed.

Calculate Monthly Water Consumption

	A	B	C	D	E
1	Department	Daily Consumption (Liters)			
2	HR	120	HR	3600 liters	
3	Engineering	300	Engineering	9000 liters	
4	Marketing	150	Marketing	4500 liters	
5	Sales	130	Sales	3900 liters	
6	Production	500	Production	15000 liters	

Objective: Develop a function to calculate the monthly water consumption for different departments based on daily usage.
Sample Data:

Department	Daily Consumption (Liters)
HR	120
Engineering	300
Marketing	150
Sales	130
Production	500

Learning Outcomes:
- Learn to calculate total consumption by multiplying daily usage by the number of days in the month.
- Practice basic arithmetic operations in an environmental management context.

Code Example:

```
/**
 * Calculates monthly water consumption for each
department.
 *
 * @param {range} departments The range containing
department names.
 * @param {range} dailyConsumption The range containing
daily water consumption in liters.
 * @return {array | string} An array listing each department
with its monthly water consumption, assuming a 30-day
month, or an error message if data is invalid.
 * @customfunction
 */
function
CALCULATE_MONTHLY_WATER_CONSUMPTION(depar
tments, dailyConsumption) {
const daysInMonth = 30; // Assuming 30 days in the month
const results = [];
for (let i = 0; i < departments.length; i++) {
const department = departments[i][0];
const daily = dailyConsumption[i][0];
const monthlyConsumption = daily * daysInMonth;
results.push([department, monthlyConsumption + " liters"]);
}
return results.length > 0 ? results : "Invalid or empty data!";
}
```

Steps:

1. Paste the code into a new Apps Script project.
2. Save the changes and return to Google Sheets.
3. Enter the sample data into columns A1:B6.
4. Use the function like
   =CALCULATE_MONTHLY_WATER_CONSUMPTI
   ON(A2:A6, B2:B6).

Expected Result: The function will calculate and list the monthly water consumption for each department, providing insight into resource usage and helping to manage environmental impacts.

Summarize Client Feedback Scores

A5	▼	fx =SUMMARIZE_CLIENT_FEEDBACK(A2:A4, B2:D4)		
	A	B	C	D
1	Service	Client 1 Score	Client 2 Score	Client 3 Score
2	Consulting	4	5	4
3	Training	5	4	5
4	Support	3	4	4
5	Consulting	4.33		
6	Training	4.67		
7	Support	3.67		

Objective: Create a function to summarize feedback scores by calculating the average score given by clients for each service offered.

Sample Data:

Service	Client 1 Score	Client 2 Score	Client 3 Score
Consulting	4	5	4
Training	5	4	5
Support	3	4	4

Learning Outcomes:
- Learn to aggregate scores and calculate averages for different services.
- Practice manipulating and summarizing data to assess service quality.

Code Example:

```
/**
* Summarizes client feedback scores by calculating the average score for each service.
*
* @param {range} services The range containing service names.
```

```
 * @param {range} scores The range containing feedback
scores from multiple clients.
 * @return {array | string} An array summarizing the average
feedback score for each service, or an error message if data is
invalid.
 * @customfunction
 */
function SUMMARIZE_CLIENT_FEEDBACK(services,
scores) {
 const results = [];
 for (let i = 0; i < services.length; i++) {
  const service = services[i][0];
  let totalScore = 0;
  let count = 0;
  for (let j = 0; j < scores[i].length; j++) {
  totalScore += scores[i][j];
  count++;
  }
  const averageScore = (totalScore / count).toFixed(2);
  results.push([service, averageScore]);
 }
 return results.length > 0 ? results : "Invalid or empty data!";
}
```

Steps:
1. Paste the code into a new Apps Script project.
2. Save the changes and return to Google Sheets.
3. Enter the sample data into a grid format from A1:D4.
4. Use the function like
   =SUMMARIZE_CLIENT_FEEDBACK(A2:A4, B2:D4).

Expected Result: The function will calculate and list the average feedback score for each service, providing valuable insights into client satisfaction and service performance.

Analyze Sales Trends by Product

	A	B	C	D	E
1	Product	Q1 Sales	Q2 Sales		
2	Laptop	150	200	Laptop	Increase
3	Smartphone	250	230	Smartphone	Decrease
4	Tablet	100	120	Tablet	Increase
5	Camera	80	90	Camera	Increase
6	Headphones	200	210	Headphones	Increase

Objective: Develop a function to analyze quarterly sales trends for products by comparing sales figures across two quarters.

Sample Data:

Product	Q1 Sales	Q2 Sales
Laptop	150	200
Smartphone	250	230
Tablet	100	120
Camera	80	90
Headphones	200	210

Learning Outcomes:
- Learn to compare numerical data to identify trends (increase, decrease, or stable).
- Practice using arithmetic comparisons to generate insightful business analytics.

Code Example:

```
/**
 * Analyzes quarterly sales trends by product.
 *
 * @param {range} products The range containing product names.
 * @param {range} q1Sales The range containing Q1 sales figures.
 * @param {range} q2Sales The range containing Q2 sales figures.
```

* @return {array | string} An array listing each product with its sales trend ("Increase", "Decrease", "Stable"), or an error message if data is invalid.
* @customfunction
*/

```
function ANALYZE_SALES_TRENDS(products, q1Sales, q2Sales) {
 const results = [];
for (let i = 0; i < products.length; i++) {
 const product = products[i][0];
 const salesQ1 = q1Sales[i][0];
 const salesQ2 = q2Sales[i][0];
 const trend = salesQ2 > salesQ1 ? "Increase" : salesQ2 < salesQ1 ? "Decrease" : "Stable";
 results.push([product, trend]);
 }
 return results.length > 0 ? results : "No sales data to analyze.";
}
```

Steps:
1. Paste the code into a new Apps Script project.
2. Save the changes and return to Google Sheets.
3. Enter the sample data into columns A1:C6.
4. Use the function like
   =ANALYZE_SALES_TRENDS(A2:A6, B2:B6, C2:C6).

Expected Result: The function will return an array listing each product along with its sales trend between the two quarters.

Summarize Employee Skills Proficiency

	A	B	C	D	E
1	Department	Employee Name	Proficiency Rating		
2	Sales	John	4	Sales	4.00
3	Sales	Emily	3	Marketing	3.33
4	Sales	Michael	5	HR	4.50
5	Sales	Sarah	4		
6	Marketing	David	3		
7	Marketing	Emma	4		
8	Marketing	Sophia	3		
9	HR	Daniel	5		
10	HR	Olivia	4		
11	HR	Ava	3		

Objective: Create a function to summarize the average proficiency rating of employee skills in a department.

Sample Data:

Department	Employee Name	Proficiency Rating
Sales	John	4
Sales	Emily	3
Sales	Michael	5
Sales	Sarah	4
Marketing	David	3
Marketing	Emma	4
Marketing	Sophia	3
HR	Daniel	5
HR	Olivia	4
HR	Ava	3

Learning Outcomes:
- Learn to group and summarize data based on multiple criteria.
- Practice calculating average values for grouped data.

Code Example:

```
/**
```

* Summarizes employee skills proficiency by department.
 *
 * @param {range} departments The range containing department names.
 * @param {range} employees The range containing employee names.
 * @param {range} proficiencies The range containing skill proficiency ratings.
 * @return {array | string} An array summarizing average proficiency ratings for each department, or an error message if input data is invalid.
 * @customfunction
 */

```
function
SUMMARIZE_SKILLS_PROFICIENCY(departments,
employees, proficiencies) {
 const summary = {};
for (let i = 0; i < departments.length; i++) {
 const department = departments[i][0];
 const proficiency = proficiencies[i][0];
 if (!summary[department]) {
 summary[department] = { total: 0, count: 0 };
 }
 summary[department].total += proficiency;
 summary[department].count++;
 }
 const results = [];
 Object.keys(summary).forEach(department => {
 const average = summary[department].total /
summary[department].count;
 results.push([department, average.toFixed(2)]);
 });
 return results.length > 0 ? results : "No valid data!";
}
```

Steps:
1. Paste the code into a new Apps Script project.
2. Save the changes and return to Google Sheets.

3. Enter the sample data into columns A1:C10.
4. Use the function like
   =SUMMARIZE_SKILLS_PROFICIENCY(A2:A10,
   B2:B10, C2:C10).

Expected Result: The function will compute and return the average skill proficiency rating for each department based on the provided employee data.

Convert Employee Hours to Weeks

C2	▼	fx =CONVERT_HOURS_TO_WEEKS(A2:A6, B2:B6)		
	A	B	C	D
1	Employee	Hours Worked		
2	Alice	120	Alice	3.00 weeks
3	Bob	310	Bob	7.75 weeks
4	Carol	410	Carol	10.25 weeks
5	David	210	David	5.25 weeks
6	Emily	350	Emily	8.75 weeks

Objective: Write a function to convert the total hours worked by employees into weeks, assuming a 40-hour work week.
Sample Data:

Employee	Hours Worked
Alice	120
Bob	310
Carol	410
David	210
Emily	350

Learning Outcomes:
- Learn to perform unit conversions using basic arithmetic operations.
- Practice formatting output to reflect calculated weeks of work.

Code Example:
```
/**
```

* Converts total hours worked into weeks.
*
* @param {range} employees The range containing employee names.
* @param {range} hours The range containing hours worked.
* @return {array | string} An array listing employees with their converted work weeks, or an error message if data is invalid.
* @customfunction
*/

```
function CONVERT_HOURS_TO_WEEKS(employees, hours) {
const results = [];
const hoursPerWeek = 40;
for (let i = 0; i < employees.length; i++) {
const employee = employees[i][0];
const totalHours = hours[i][0];
const weeksWorked = (totalHours /
hoursPerWeek).toFixed(2); // Formatting to two decimal places for precision
results.push([employee, weeksWorked + " weeks"]);
}
return results.length > 0 ? results : "Invalid or empty data!";
}
```

Steps:
1. Paste the code into a new Apps Script project.
2. Save the changes and return to Google Sheets.
3. Enter the sample data into columns A1:B6.
4. Use the function like
   =CONVERT_HOURS_TO_WEEKS(A2:A6, B2:B6).

Expected Result: The function will return each employee's name along with the equivalent number of weeks worked, based on their total hours.

Filter Products by Price Range

| C2 | ▼ | f_x =FILTER_PRODUCTS_BY_PRICE(A2:A6, B2:B6, 1, 20) |

	A	B	C	D
1	Product	Price		
2	Notebook	9.99	Notebook	$9.99
3	Pen	1.2	Pen	$1.20
4	Pencil	0.5	Calculator	$19.99
5	Backpack	49.99		
6	Calculator	19.99		

Objective: Develop a function to list products that fall within a specified price range.

Sample Data:

Product	Price
Notebook	9.99
Pen	1.2
Pencil	0.5
Backpack	49.99
Calculator	19.99

Learning Outcomes:
- Practice using conditional logic to filter data based on given criteria.
- Learn to handle range-based filtering in a dataset.

Code Example:

```
/**
 * Lists products within a specified price range.
 *
 * @param {range} products The range containing product
names.
 * @param {range} prices The range containing product prices.
 * @param {number} minPrice The minimum price of the
range.
 * @param {number} maxPrice The maximum price of the
range.
 * @return {array | string} An array listing products within the
price range, or an error message if no products are found.
 * @customfunction
```

```
*/
function FILTER_PRODUCTS_BY_PRICE(products, prices,
minPrice, maxPrice) {
 const filteredProducts = [];
 for (let i = 0; i < products.length; i++) {
 const product = products[i][0];
 const price = prices[i][0];
 if (price >= minPrice && price <= maxPrice) {
 filteredProducts.push([product, "$" + price.toFixed(2)]);
 }
 }
 return filteredProducts.length > 0 ? filteredProducts : "No
products in the specified price range.";
}
```

Steps:
1. Paste the code into a new Apps Script project.
2. Save the changes and return to Google Sheets.
3. Enter the sample data into columns A1:B6.
4. Use the function like
   =FILTER_PRODUCTS_BY_PRICE(A2:A6, B2:B6, 1,
   20).

Expected Result: The function will list all products whose
prices fall within the specified range ($1 to $20).

Summarize Sales by Year and Category

D2	▼	fx =SUMMARIZE_SALES_BY_YEAR_CATEGORY(A2:A6, B2:B6, C2:C6)				
	A	B	C	D	E	F
1	Year	Category	Sales			
2	2023	Tech	150000	2023	Tech	150000
3	2023	Home	80000	2023	Home	80000
4	2024	Tech	180000	2024	Tech	180000
5	2024	Home	90000	2024	Home	90000
6	2024	Garden	50000	2024	Garden	50000

Objective: Create a function to summarize total sales by year
and category from a sales record dataset.

Sample Data:

Year	Category	Sales
2023	Tech	150000

2023	Home	80000
2024	Tech	180000
2024	Home	90000
2024	Garden	50000

Learning Outcomes:

- Learn to aggregate and summarize data based on multiple grouping criteria.
- Practice complex data manipulation tasks involving sums and groups.

Code Example:

```
/**
 * Summarizes sales by year and category.
 *
 * @param {range} years The range containing year data.
 * @param {range} categories The range containing category
names.
 * @param {range} sales The range containing sales figures.
 * @return {array | string} An array summarizing sales by year
and category, or an error message if data is invalid.
 * @customfunction
 */
function
SUMMARIZE_SALES_BY_YEAR_CATEGORY(years,
categories, sales) {
 const salesSummary = {};
 for (let i = 0; i < years.length; i++) {
 const year = years[i][0];
 const category = categories[i][0];
 const sale = sales[i][0];
 if (!salesSummary[year]) salesSummary[year] = {};
 if (!salesSummary[year][category])
salesSummary[year][category] = 0;
 salesSummary[year][category] += sale;
 }
 const results = [];
 Object.keys(salesSummary).forEach(year => {
```

```
Object.keys(salesSummary[year]).forEach(category => {
  results.push([year, category,
salesSummary[year][category]]);
});
});
return results.length > 0 ? results : "No sales data to
summarize.";
}
```

Steps:
1. Paste the code into a new Apps Script project.
2. Save the changes and return to Google Sheets.
3. Enter the sample data into columns A1:C6.
4. Use the function like
   =SUMMARIZE_SALES_BY_YEAR_CATEGORY(A2:A
   6, B2:B6, C2:C6).

Expected Result: The function will provide a summary of total sales, organized by year and category, displaying how each category performed in each year.

Calculate Project Cost Overruns

A1:C6   ▾ | *fx* Project

	A	B	C	D	E
1	Project	Budgeted Cost	Actual Cost		
2	Project A	50000	55000	Project A	5000
3	Project B	40000	39000	Project C	5000
4	Project C	75000	80000	Project E	5000
5	Project D	60000	60000		
6	Project E	45000	50000		

Objective: Write a function to calculate project cost overruns by comparing actual costs to budgeted costs.

Sample Data:

Project	Budgeted Cost	Actual Cost
Project A	50000	55000
Project B	40000	39000
Project C	75000	80000

Project D	60000	60000
Project E	45000	50000

Learning Outcomes:

- Learn to calculate differences between two sets of numbers.
- Practice identifying and quantifying financial variances.

Code Example:

```
/**
 * Calculates cost overruns for projects.
 *
 * @param {range} projects The range containing project
names.
 * @param {range} budgetedCosts The range containing
budgeted costs.
 * @param {range} actualCosts The range containing actual
costs.
 * @return {array | string} An array listing projects with their
cost overruns, or an error message if no overruns are found.
 * @customfunction
 */
function CALCULATE_COST_OVERRUNS(projects,
budgetedCosts, actualCosts) {
 const results = [];
 for (let i = 0; i < projects.length; i++) {
 const project = projects[i][0];
 const budgetedCost = budgetedCosts[i][0];
 const actualCost = actualCosts[i][0];
 const overrun = actualCost - budgetedCost;
 if (overrun > 0) {
 results.push([project, overrun]);
 }
 }
 return results.length > 0 ? results : "No cost overruns
detected.";
}
```

Steps:

1. Paste the code into a new Apps Script project.
2. Save the changes and return to Google Sheets.
3. Enter the sample data into columns A1:C6.
4. Use the function like =CALCULATE_COST_OVERRUNS(A2:A6, B2:B6, C2:C6).

Expected Result: The function will return a list of projects that exceeded their budget along with the amount of each overrun.

Analyze Sales Performance by Region

D2	▾	fx =ANALYZE_SALES_PERFORMANCE(A2:A6, B2:B6, C2:C6)			
	A	B	C	D	E
1	Region	Sales	Target		
2	North	10500	10000	North	Above Target
3	South	9500	10000	South	Below Target
4	East	10000	10000	East	On Target
5	West	15000	12000	West	Above Target
6	Central	8000	9000	Central	Below Target

Objective: Develop a function to analyze sales performance by region, classifying them as "Above Target", "On Target", or "Below Target" based on a specified sales target.

Sample Data:

Region	Sales	Target
North	10500	10000
South	9500	10000
East	10000	10000
West	15000	12000
Central	8000	9000

Learning Outcomes:

- Learn to compare sales figures against targets to classify performance.
- Practice using conditional logic to categorize data.

Code Example:

```
/**
```

* Analyzes sales performance by region against set targets.
*
* @param {range} regions The range containing region names.
* @param {range} sales The range containing sales figures.
* @param {range} targets The range containing sales targets.
* @return {array | string} An array listing each region with its performance status, or an error message if input data is invalid.
* @customfunction
*/

```
function ANALYZE_SALES_PERFORMANCE(regions, sales, targets) {
const results = [];
for (let i = 0; i < regions.length; i++) {
const region = regions[i][0];
const sale = sales[i][0];
const target = targets[i][0];
const status = sale > target ? "Above Target" : sale === target ? "On Target" : "Below Target";
results.push([region, status]);
}
return results.length > 0 ? results : "No sales data to analyze.";
}
```

Steps:
1. Paste the code into a new Apps Script project.
2. Save the changes and return to Google Sheets.
3. Enter the sample data into columns A1:C6.
4. Use the function like =ANALYZE_SALES_PERFORMANCE(A2:A6, B2:B6, C2:C6).

Expected Result: The function will classify each region's sales performance relative to its target, providing insights into which regions are performing above, on, or below expectations.

Summarize Customer Feedback Scores

C2	▾	_fx_ =SUMMARIZE_FEEDBACK_SCORES(A2:A6, B2:B6)		
	A	B	C	D
1	Feedback Type	Score		
2	Service	8	Service	8.5
3	Product	7	Product	7.5
4	Delivery	9	Delivery	9.0
5	Service	9		
6	Product	8		

Objective: Create a function to summarize customer feedback scores, calculating the average score for each feedback category.

Sample Data:

Feedback Type	Score
Service	8
Product	7
Delivery	9
Service	9
Product	8

Learning Outcomes:

- Learn to aggregate scores and calculate averages for different categories.
- Practice manipulating and summarizing data for reporting purposes.

Code Example:

```
/**
* Summarizes customer feedback scores by type.
*
* @param {range} types The range containing feedback types.
* @param {range} scores The range containing feedback scores.
* @return {array | string} An array listing each feedback type with its average score, or an error message if input data is invalid.
* @customfunction
*/
```

```
function SUMMARIZE_FEEDBACK_SCORES(types, scores) {
const feedbackSummary = {};
for (let i = 0; i < types.length; i++) {
const type = types[i][0];
const score = scores[i][0];
if (!feedbackSummary[type]) {
feedbackSummary[type] = { total: 0, count: 0 };
}
feedbackSummary[type].total += score;
feedbackSummary[type].count++;
}
const results = [];
Object.keys(feedbackSummary).forEach(type => {
const average = (feedbackSummary[type].total /
feedbackSummary[type].count).toFixed(1);
results.push([type, average]);
});
return results.length > 0 ? results : "No feedback data
available.";
}
```

Steps:
1. Paste the code into a new Apps Script project.
2. Save the changes and return to Google Sheets.
3. Enter the sample data into columns A1:B6.
4. Use the function like
   =SUMMARIZE_FEEDBACK_SCORES(A2:A6, B2:B6).

Expected Result: The function will calculate and return the average feedback score for each category, helping to gauge customer satisfaction across different aspects of the business.

Evaluate Employee Overtime Hours

C2	▾	_fx_ =EVALUATE_OVERTIME(A2:A6, B2:B6, 10)		
	A	B	C	D
1	Employee	Overtime Hours		
2	Alice	12	Alice	12
3	Bob	8	Carol	15
4	Carol	15	Emily	20
5	David	5		
6	Emily	20		

Objective: Write a function to evaluate and list employees who have exceeded a specific threshold of overtime hours in a month.

Sample Data:

Employee	Overtime Hours
Alice	12
Bob	8
Carol	15
David	5
Emily	20

Learning Outcomes:
- Learn to filter data based on a specific numerical threshold.
- Practice using conditional logic to identify and list specific data points.

Code Example:

```
/**
* Evaluates and lists employees with overtime hours
exceeding a set threshold.
*
* @param {range} employees The range containing employee
names.
* @param {range} overtimeHours The range containing
overtime hours worked.
* @param {number} threshold The overtime hours threshold.
```

```
 * @return {array | string} An array listing employees who
have exceeded the overtime threshold, or an error message if
no employees have exceeded the threshold.
 * @customfunction
 */
function EVALUATE_OVERTIME(employees,
overtimeHours, threshold) {
 const results = [];
 for (let i = 0; i < employees.length; i++) {
 const employee = employees[i][0];
 const hours = overtimeHours[i][0];
 if (hours > threshold) {
 results.push([employee, hours]);
 }
 }
 return results.length > 0 ? results : "No employees have
exceeded the overtime threshold.";
}
```

Steps:

1. Paste the code into a new Apps Script project.
2. Save the changes and return to Google Sheets.
3. Enter the sample data into columns A1:B6.
4. Use the function like
   =EVALUATE_OVERTIME(A2:A6, B2:B6, 10).

Expected Result: The function will return a list of employees
who have exceeded 10 overtime hours in a month, along with
the number of hours they worked.

Summarize Product Sales by Month

D2   ▼   ƒx =SUMMARIZE_SALES_BY_MONTH(A2:A7, B2:B7, C2:C7)

	A	B	C	D	E	F
1	Month	Product	Sales			
2	January	Notebook	300	January	Notebook	300
3	January	Pen	150	January	Pen	150
4	February	Notebook	200	February	Notebook	200
5	February	Pen	100	February	Pen	100
6	March	Notebook	400	March	Notebook	400
7	March	Pen	120	March	Pen	120

Objective: Develop a function to summarize total sales for each product by month.

Sample Data:

Month	Product	Sales
January	Notebook	300
January	Pen	150
February	Notebook	200
February	Pen	100
March	Notebook	400
March	Pen	120

Learning Outcomes:
- Learn to aggregate and summarize data based on multiple grouping criteria.
- Practice complex data manipulation tasks involving sums and groups.

Code Example:

```
/**
 * Summarizes product sales by month.
 *
 * @param {range} months The range containing month
names.
 * @param {range} products The range containing product
names.
 * @param {range} sales The range containing sales figures.
 * @return {array | string} An array summarizing total sales for
each product by month, or an error message if data is invalid.
 * @customfunction
 */
function SUMMARIZE_SALES_BY_MONTH(months,
products, sales) {
 const summary = {};
 for (let i = 0; i < months.length; i++) {
 const month = months[i][0];
 const product = products[i][0];
```

```
const sale = sales[i][0];
if (!summary[month]) summary[month] = {};
if (!summary[month][product]) summary[month][product] =
0;
summary[month][product] += sale;
}
const results = [];
Object.keys(summary).forEach(month => {
Object.keys(summary[month]).forEach(product => {
results.push([month, product, summary[month][product]]);
});
});
return results.length > 0 ? results : "No sales data to
summarize.";
}
```

Steps:
1. Paste the code into a new Apps Script project.
2. Save the changes and return to Google Sheets.
3. Enter the sample data into columns A1:C7.
4. Use the function like
   =SUMMARIZE_SALES_BY_MONTH(A2:A7, B2:B7,
   C2:C7).

Expected Result: The function will provide a summary of total sales, organized by month and product, displaying how each product performed in each month.

Classify Customer Complaints by Urgency

C2	▾	fx =CLASSIFY_COMPLAINTS_BY_URGENCY(A2:A6, B2:B6)		
	A	B	C	D
1	Complaint ID	Description		
2	C001	"Need immediate attention to my account."	C001	High Urgency
3	C002	"Please address this issue when possible."	C002	Normal Urgency
4	C003	"It is urgent that this is resolved."	C003	High Urgency
5	C004	"General inquiry, no rush."	C004	Normal Urgency
6	C005	"Need this fixed ASAP."	C005	High Urgency

Objective: Create a function to classify customer complaints based on urgency keywords such as "immediate", "urgent", or "as soon as possible".

Sample Data:

Complaint ID	Description
C001	"Need immediate attention to my account."
C002	"Please address this issue when possible."
C003	"It is urgent that this is resolved."
C004	"General inquiry, no rush."
C005	"Need this fixed ASAP."

Learning Outcomes:

- Learn to apply simple text analysis for urgency classification.
- Practice string manipulations and conditional logic.

Code Example:

```
/**
* Classifies customer complaints based on urgency.
*
* @param {range} complaintIDs The range containing
complaint IDs.
* @param {range} descriptions The range containing
descriptions of each complaint.
* @return {array | string} An array classifying each complaint
by urgency level, or an error message if no complaints meet
urgency criteria.
* @customfunction
*/
function
CLASSIFY_COMPLAINTS_BY_URGENCY(complaintIDs,
descriptions) {
 const urgencyKeywords = ["immediate", "urgent", "as soon
as possible", "asap"];
 const classifiedComplaints = [];
for (let i = 0; i < complaintIDs.length; i++) {
 const id = complaintIDs[i][0];
 const description = descriptions[i][0].toLowerCase();
 const isUrgent = urgencyKeywords.some(keyword =>
description.includes(keyword));
```

classifiedComplaints.push([id, isUrgent ? "High Urgency" :
"Normal Urgency"]);
}
return classifiedComplaints.length > 0 ? classifiedComplaints
: "No complaints classified as urgent.";
}

Steps:
1. Paste the code into a new Apps Script project.
2. Save the changes and return to Google Sheets.
3. Enter the sample data into columns A1:B6.
4. Use the function like
   =CLASSIFY_COMPLAINTS_BY_URGENCY(A2:A6,
   B2:B6).

Expected Result: The function will classify each complaint based on the urgency indicated in the description, aiding in prioritization of customer service responses.

Calculate Monthly Energy Consumption

C2	▾	*fx* =CALCULATE_MONTHLY_ENERGY(A2:A6, B2:B6, 30)		
	A	B	C	D
1	Department	Daily Usage (kWh)		
2	Operations	320	Operations	9600
3	Marketing	280	Marketing	8400
4	Development	450	Development	13500
5	HR	125	HR	3750
6	Sales	310	Sales	9300

Objective: Write a function to calculate the total monthly energy consumption for different departments based on daily usage.

Sample Data:

Department	Daily Usage (kWh)
Operations	320
Marketing	280
Development	450
HR	125

Sales	310

Learning Outcomes:

- Learn to calculate total consumption by multiplying daily usage by the number of days in the month.
- Practice basic arithmetic operations in a practical scenario.

Code Example:

```
/**
 * Calculates the monthly energy consumption for each
department.
 *
 * @param {range} departments The range containing
department names.
 * @param {range} dailyUsages The range containing daily
energy usage in kWh.
 * @param {number} daysInMonth The number of days in the
month.
 * @return {array | string} An array listing each department
with its monthly energy consumption, or an error message if
data is invalid.
 * @customfunction
 */
function CALCULATE_MONTHLY_ENERGY(departments,
dailyUsages, daysInMonth) {
 const results = [];
for (let i = 0; i < departments.length; i++) {
 const department = departments[i][0];
 const dailyUsage = dailyUsages[i][0];
 const monthlyConsumption = dailyUsage * daysInMonth;
 results.push([department, monthlyConsumption]);
 }
 return results.length > 0 ? results : "Invalid or empty data!";
}
```

Steps:

1. Paste the code into a new Apps Script project.
2. Save the changes and return to Google Sheets.

3. Enter the sample data into columns A1:B6.
4. Use the function like
=CALCULATE_MONTHLY_ENERGY(A2:A6, B2:B6, 30) for a 30-day month.

Expected Result: The function will return the total monthly energy consumption for each department.

12 : Ranking and sorting outputs

In this chapter examples will calculate, and compute output results into the blank data cells.

Rank Students by Grades

C2	▼	_fx_ =RANK_STUDENTS_BY_GRADES(A2:A6, B2:B6)		
	A	B	C	D
1	Student	Grade		
2	Alice	88	Bob	95
3	Bob	95	David	91
4	Carol	82	Alice	88
5	David	91	Carol	82
6	Emily	78	Emily	78

Objective: Develop a function to rank students based on their grades from highest to lowest.

Sample Data:

Student	Grade
Alice	88
Bob	95
Carol	82
David	91
Emily	78

Learning Outcomes:
- Learn to sort data based on numerical values.
- Practice array manipulations and sorting techniques.

Code Example:

```
/**
 * Ranks students by their grades.
 *
 * @param {range} students The range containing student
 names.
 * @param {range} grades The range containing student
 grades.
 * @return {array | string} An array listing students ranked by
 their grades from highest to lowest, or an error message if
 data is invalid.
 * @customfunction
 */
function RANK_STUDENTS_BY_GRADES(students, grades)
{
 const studentGrades = [];
 for (let i = 0; i < students.length; i++) {
 studentGrades.push({name: students[i][0], grade:
 grades[i][0]});
 }
 studentGrades.sort((a, b) => b.grade - a.grade);
 const results = studentGrades.map(item => [item.name,
 item.grade]);
 return results.length > 0 ? results : "Invalid or empty data!";
}
```

Steps:
1. Paste the code into a new Apps Script project.
2. Save the changes and return to Google Sheets.
3. Enter the sample data into columns A1:B6.
4. Use the function like
   =RANK_STUDENTS_BY_GRADES(A2:A6, B2:B6).

Expected Result: The function will return a list of students ranked by their grades from highest to lowest.

Identify Overdue Tasks

C2   ▾   _fx_ =IDENTIFY_OVERDUE_TASKS(A2:A6, B2:B6)

	A	B	C	D
1	Task	Due Date		
2	Task 1	2024-04-01	Task 1	2024-04-01
3	Task 2	2024-04-15	Task 2	2024-04-15
4	Task 3	2024-03-30	Task 3	2024-03-30
5	Task 4	2024-04-10	Task 4	2024-04-10
6	Task 5	2024-03-25	Task 5	2024-03-25

Objective: Create a function to identify tasks that are overdue based on their due dates.

Sample Data:

Task	Due Date
Task 1	2024-04-01
Task 2	2024-04-15
Task 3	2024-03-30
Task 4	2024-04-10
Task 5	2024-03-25

Learning Outcomes:

- Learn to compare dates to determine if tasks are overdue.
- Practice using date functions and conditional logic.

Code Example:

```
/**
 * Identifies overdue tasks based on their due dates.
 *
 * @param {range} tasks The range containing task names.
 * @param {range} dueDates The range containing task due
dates.
 * @return {array | string} An array listing overdue tasks, or an
error message if no tasks are overdue.
 * @customfunction
 */
function IDENTIFY_OVERDUE_TASKS(tasks, dueDates) {
  const today = new Date();
```

```
const results = [];
for (let i = 0; i < tasks.length; i++) {
const task = tasks[i][0];
const dueDate = new Date(dueDates[i][0]);
if (dueDate < today) {
results.push([task, dueDate.toISOString().split('T')[0]]);
}
}
return results.length > 0 ? results : "No overdue tasks.";
}
```

Steps:

1. Paste the code into a new Apps Script project.
2. Save the changes and return to Google Sheets.
3. Enter the sample data into columns A1:B6.
4. Adjust the system date for testing, if necessary, and use the function like
   =IDENTIFY_OVERDUE_TASKS(A2:A6, B2:B6).

Expected Result: The function will identify and list any tasks that are overdue based on their due dates.

Compute Weighted Grade Averages

D2 ▾ | *fx* =WEIGHTED_GRADE_AVERAGES(A2:A6, B2:B6, C2:C6)

	A	B	C	D	E
1	Student	Assignment 1 (40%)	Assignment 2 (60%)		
2	Alice	85	90	Alice	88.00
3	Bob	78	84	Bob	81.60
4	Carol	92	88	Carol	89.60
5	David	75	80	David	78.00
6	Emily	88	91	Emily	89.80

Objective: Write a function to compute the weighted average grade for students based on multiple assignments, where each assignment has a different weight towards the final grade.

Sample Data:

Student	Assignment 1 (40%)	Assignment 2 (60%)

Alice	85	90	–
Bob	78	84	
Carol	92	88	
David	75	80	
Emily	88	91	

Learning Outcomes:

- Learn to calculate weighted averages.
- Practice applying percentages to actual values to achieve a computed result.

Code Example:

```
/**
 * Computes the weighted average grade for students.
 *
 * @param {range} students The range containing student
names.
 * @param {range} grades1 The range containing grades for
Assignment 1.
 * @param {range} grades2 The range containing grades for
Assignment 2.
 * @return {array | string} An array listing each student with
their weighted average grade, or an error message if data is
invalid.
 * @customfunction
 */
function WEIGHTED_GRADE_AVERAGES(students,
grades1, grades2) {
const results = [];
for (let i = 0; i < students.length; i++) {
const student = students[i][0];
const grade1 = grades1[i][0];
const grade2 = grades2[i][0];
const weightedAverage = (grade1 * 0.4) + (grade2 * 0.6);
results.push([student, weightedAverage.toFixed(2)]);
}
return results.length > 0 ? results : "Invalid or empty data!";
```

}

Steps:

1. Paste the code into a new Apps Script project.
2. Save the changes and return to Google Sheets.
3. Enter the sample data into columns A1:C6.
4. Use the function like
   =WEIGHTED_GRADE_AVERAGES(A2:A6, B2:B6, C2:C6).

Expected Result: The function will calculate and return each student's weighted average grade based on the grades and their respective weights for the two assignments.

List Products Below Minimum Stock Levels

D2	▾	fx =LIST_PRODUCTS_BELOW_MIN_STOCK(A2:A6, B2:B6, C2:C6)		
	A	B	C	D	E
1	Product	Current Stock	Minimum Stock Level		
2	Pen	150	200	Pen	150
3	Notebook	300	250	Eraser	100
4	Eraser	100	150		
5	Marker	80	75		
6	Pencil	60	50		

Objective: Develop a function to identify and list products that are below the minimum required stock levels.

Sample Data:

Product	Current Stock	Minimum Stock Level
Pen	150	200
Notebook	300	250
Eraser	100	150
Marker	80	75
Pencil	60	50

Learning Outcomes:

- Learn to compare numerical data to identify discrepancies.
- Practice using conditional statements to filter data.

Code Example:

```
/**
* Lists products that are below minimum stock levels.
*
* @param {range} products The range containing product names.
* @param {range} currentStocks The range containing current stock quantities.
* @param {range} minimumStocks The range containing minimum stock levels.
* @return {array | string} An array listing products below minimum stock levels, or an error message if all products meet stock requirements.
* @customfunction
*/
function LIST_PRODUCTS_BELOW_MIN_STOCK(products, currentStocks, minimumStocks) {
const results = [];
for (let i = 0; i < products.length; i++) {
const product = products[i][0];
const currentStock = currentStocks[i][0];
const minimumStock = minimumStocks[i][0];
if (currentStock < minimumStock) {
results.push([product, currentStock]);
}
}
return results.length > 0 ? results : "All products meet or exceed minimum stock levels.";
}
```

Steps:
1. Paste the code into a new Apps Script project.
2. Save the changes and return to Google Sheets.
3. Enter the sample data into columns A1:C6.

4. Use the function like
   =LIST_PRODUCTS_BELOW_MIN_STOCK(A2:A6,
   B2:B6, C2:C6).

Expected Result: The function will identify and list products that are below their specified minimum stock levels, including their current stock.

Calculate Monthly Growth Rate

C2	▼	ƒx =CALCULATE_MONTHLY_GROWTH_RATE(A2:A6, B2:B6)		
	A	B	C	D
1	Month	Sales		
2	January	10000	February	5.00%
3	February	10500	March	4.76%
4	March	11000	April	4.55%
5	April	11500	May	4.35%
6	May	12000		

Objective: Create a function to calculate the monthly growth rate for a series of monthly sales figures.

Sample Data:

Month	Sales
January	10000
February	10500
March	11000
April	11500
May	12000

Learning Outcomes:
- Learn to calculate percentage growth between consecutive data points.
- Practice handling sequential data and calculating changes over time.

Code Example:
```
/**
* Calculates the monthly growth rate for sales.
*
```

* @param {range} months The range containing month names.

* @param {range} sales The range containing monthly sales figures.

* @return {array | string} An array listing each month with its growth rate compared to the previous month, or an error message if data is invalid.

* @customfunction

*/

```javascript
function
CALCULATE_MONTHLY_GROWTH_RATE(months, sales)
{
  const results = [];
  for (let i = 1; i < sales.length; i++) {
    const month = months[i][0];
    const previousSales = sales[i - 1][0];
    const currentSales = sales[i][0];
    const growthRate = ((currentSales - previousSales) /
    previousSales) * 100;
    results.push([month, growthRate.toFixed(2) + "%"]);
  }
  return results.length > 0 ? results : "Insufficient data for
  growth calculation.";
}
```

Steps:

1. Paste the code into a new Apps Script project.
2. Save the changes and return to Google Sheets.
3. Enter the sample data into columns A1:B6.
4. Use the function like
   =CALCULATE_MONTHLY_GROWTH_RATE(A2:A6
   , B2:B6).

Expected Result: The function will calculate the growth rate for each month compared to the previous month, providing insights into sales dynamics.

Assess Employee Training Completion

Objective: Develop a function to list employees who have not completed mandatory training courses.

Sample Data:

Employee	Training Completed
Alice	Yes
Bob	No
Carol	Yes
David	No
Emily	Yes

Learning Outcomes:

- Learn to filter and identify specific entries based on a condition.
- Practice using boolean logic to handle categorical data.

Code Example:

```
/**
* Lists employees who have not completed mandatory
training.
*
* @param {range} employees The range containing employee
names.
```

* @param {range} trainingStatus The range indicating if training was completed ('Yes' or 'No').
* @return {array | string} An array listing employees who have not completed training, or an error message if all have completed.
* @customfunction
*/

```
function LIST_INCOMPLETE_TRAINING(employees,
trainingStatus) {
 const results = [];
for (let i = 0; i < employees.length; i++) {
 const employee = employees[i][0];
 const completed = trainingStatus[i][0];
 if (completed === "No") {
 results.push([employee]);
 }
 }
 return results.length > 0 ? results : "All employees have
completed the training.";
}
```

Steps:
1. Paste the code into a new Apps Script project.
2. Save the changes and return to Google Sheets.
3. Enter the sample data into columns A1:B6.
4. Use the function like
   =LIST_INCOMPLETE_TRAINING(A2:A6, B2:B6).

Expected Result: The function will return a list of employees who have not completed their mandatory training.

Calculate Budget Variance

	A	B	C	D	E	F
1	Department	Budgeted Amount	Actual Spending			
2	HR	20000	19500	HR	Under Budget	-500
3	Marketing	15000	16000	Marketing	Over Budget	1000
4	Sales	18000	18000	Sales	On Budget	0
5	IT	22000	21000	IT	Under Budget	-1000
6	Finance	17000	17000	Finance	On Budget	0

Objective: Write a function to calculate budget variance for each department, indicating whether they are under or over budget.

Sample Data:

Department	Budgeted Amount	Actual Spending
HR	20000	19500
Marketing	15000	16000
Sales	18000	18000
IT	22000	21000
Finance	17000	17000

Learning Outcomes:
- Practice calculating differences between two numerical values.
- Learn to interpret and categorize results as under or over budget.

Code Example:
```
/**
 * Calculates budget variance for each department.
 *
 * @param {range} departments The range containing department names.
 * @param {range} budgeted The range containing budgeted amounts.
 * @param {range} actual The range containing actual spending.
 * @return {array | string} An array listing each department with their budget variance, or an error message if data is invalid.
 * @customfunction
```

```
*/
function CALCULATE_BUDGET_VARIANCE(departments,
budgeted, actual) {
 const results = [];
 for (let i = 0; i < departments.length; i++) {
  const department = departments[i][0];
  const budget = budgeted[i][0];
  const spend = actual[i][0];
  const variance = spend - budget;
  const status = variance > 0 ? "Over Budget" : variance < 0 ?
"Under Budget" : "On Budget";
  results.push([department, status, variance]);
 }
 return results.length > 0 ? results : "All departments are on
budget.";
}
```

Steps:

1. Paste the code into a new Apps Script project.
2. Save the changes and return to Google Sheets.
3. Enter the sample data into columns A1:C6.
4. Use the function like
   =CALCULATE_BUDGET_VARIANCE(A2:A6, B2:B6,
   C2:C6).

Expected Result: The function will return each department's budget status, indicating whether they are under, over, or on budget.

Generate Monthly Sales Reports

D2   ▼   fx =GENERATE_MONTHLY_SALES_REPORTS(A2:A7, B2:B7, C2:C7)

	A	B	C	D	E	F
1	Month	Category	Sales			
2	January	Electronics	15000	January	Electronics	15000
3	January	Apparel	8000	January	Apparel	8000
4	February	Electronics	20000	February	Electronics	20000
5	February	Apparel	12000	February	Apparel	12000
6	March	Electronics	25000	March	Electronics	25000
7	March	Apparel	10000	March	Apparel	10000

Objective: Create a function to generate a sales report summarizing total sales for each product category per month.

Sample Data:

Month	Category	Sales
January	Electronics	15000
January	Apparel	8000
February	Electronics	20000
February	Apparel	12000
March	Electronics	25000
March	Apparel	10000

Learning Outcomes:
- Learn to aggregate sales data across categories and months.
- Practice creating summary reports from detailed data records.

Code Example:

```
/**
 * Generates a monthly sales report for each product category.
 *
 * @param {range} months The range containing month names.
 * @param {range} categories The range containing product categories.
 * @param {range} sales The range containing sales figures.
 * @return {array | string} An array summarizing total sales by month and category, or an error message if data is invalid.
 * @customfunction
 */
function
GENERATE_MONTHLY_SALES_REPORTS(months, categories, sales) {
 const summary = {};
 for (let i = 0; i < months.length; i++) {
 const month = months[i][0];
 const category = categories[i][0];
 const sale = sales[i][0];
```

```
if (!summary[month]) summary[month] = {};
if (!summary[month][category]) summary[month][category]
= 0;
summary[month][category] += sale;
}
const results = [];
Object.keys(summary).forEach(month => {
Object.keys(summary[month]).forEach(category => {
results.push([month, category, summary[month][category]]);
});
});
return results.length > 0 ? results : "No sales data to
summarize.";
}
```

Steps:
1. Paste the code into a new Apps Script project.
2. Save the changes and return to Google Sheets.
3. Enter the sample data into columns A1:C7.
4. Use the function like
   =GENERATE_MONTHLY_SALES_REPORTS(A2:A7,
   B2:B7, C2:C7).

Expected Result: The function will provide a detailed report summarizing total sales for each category per month, allowing for a clear view of sales trends over time.

Compute Total Class Attendance

C2		fx =COMPUTE_TOTAL_ATTENDANCE(A2:A6, B2:B6)		
	A	B	C	D
1	Date	Students Present		
2	2024-04-01	25	119	
3	2024-04-02	23		
4	2024-04-03	24		
5	2024-04-04	22		
6	2024-04-05	25		

Objective: Write a function to compute the total attendance for classes based on daily student counts.

Sample Data:

Date	Students Present
2024-04-01	25
2024-04-02	23
2024-04-03	24
2024-04-04	22
2024-04-05	25

Learning Outcomes:

- Learn to sum up values from a range of data entries.
- Practice basic arithmetic operations in a practical context.

Code Example:

```
/**
 * Computes the total attendance for a class over a series of
days.
 *
 * @param {range} dates The range containing dates.
 * @param {range} students The range containing the number
of students present each day.
 * @return {number | string} The total number of student
attendances or an error message if data is invalid.
 * @customfunction
 */
function COMPUTE_TOTAL_ATTENDANCE(dates,
students) {
  let totalAttendance = 0;
for (let i = 0; i < students.length; i++) {
const studentCount = students[i][0];
if (typeof studentCount === 'number') {
totalAttendance += studentCount;
} else {
return "Invalid data in attendance records.";
}
```

```
}
    return totalAttendance;
}
```

Steps:

1. Paste the code into a new Apps Script project.
2. Save the changes and return to Google Sheets.
3. Enter the sample data into columns A1:B6.
4. Use the function like
   =COMPUTE_TOTAL_ATTENDANCE(A2:A6, B2:B6).

Expected Result: The function will return the total number of students present over the specified dates.

Classify Employee Performance

C2	▼	*fx* =CLASSIFY_EMPLOYEE_PERFORMANCE(A2:A6, B2:B6)	
	A	B	C	D
1	Employee	Score		
2	Alice	85	Alice	Good
3	Bob	75	Bob	Average
4	Carol	90	Carol	Excellent
5	David	65	David	Poor
6	Emily	95	Emily	Excellent

Objective: Develop a function to classify employee performance based on their evaluation scores into categories: 'Excellent', 'Good', 'Average', and 'Poor'.

Sample Data:

Employee	Score
Alice	85
Bob	75
Carol	90
David	65
Emily	95

Learning Outcomes:

- Learn to categorize numerical data into predefined groups.

- Practice using conditional logic to evaluate and assign categories.

Code Example:

```
/**
 * Classifies employee performance based on scores.
 *
 * @param {range} employees The range containing employee
 * names.
 * @param {range} scores The range containing performance
 * scores.
 * @return {array | string} An array listing each employee with
 * their performance category, or an error message if data is
 * invalid.
 * @customfunction
 */
function
CLASSIFY_EMPLOYEE_PERFORMANCE(employees,
scores) {
 const results = [];
for (let i = 0; i < employees.length; i++) {
 const employee = employees[i][0];
 let score = scores[i][0];
 let category;
 if (score >= 90) {
 category = 'Excellent';
 } else if (score >= 80) {
 category = 'Good';
 } else if (score >= 70) {
 category = 'Average';
 } else {
 category = 'Poor';
 }
 results.push([employee, category]);
 }
 return results.length > 0 ? results : "No employee scores
available.";
}
```

Steps:

1. Paste the code into a new Apps Script project.
2. Save the changes and return to Google Sheets.
3. Enter the sample data into columns A1:B6.
4. Use the function like
   =CLASSIFY_EMPLOYEE_PERFORMANCE(A2:A6, B2:B6).

Expected Result: The function will classify each employee according to their scores into 'Excellent', 'Good', 'Average', or 'Poor'.

Calculate Delivery Time Deviations

D2	▾	*fx* =CALCULATE_DELIVERY_DEVIATIONS(A2:A6, B2:B6, C2:C6)			
	A	B	C	D	E
1	Order ID	Expected Delivery Date	Actual Delivery Date		
2	1	2024-04-10	2024-04-12	1	2
3	2	2024-04-15	2024-04-14	2	-1
4	3	2024-04-20	2024-04-22	3	2
5	4	2024-04-25	2024-04-25	4	0
6	5	2024-04-30	2024-04-28	5	-2

Objective: Create a function to calculate the deviation of actual delivery times from expected times in days.

Sample Data:

Order ID	Expected Delivery Date	Actual Delivery Date
1	2024-04-10	2024-04-12
2	2024-04-15	2024-04-14
3	2024-04-20	2024-04-22
4	2024-04-25	2024-04-25
5	2024-04-30	2024-04-28

Learning Outcomes:

- Learn to compute the difference between two dates.
- Practice handling date data and performing date arithmetic.

Code Example:

```
/**
* Calculates delivery time deviations in days.
*
* @param {range} orderIDs The range containing order IDs.
* @param {range} expectedDates The range containing
expected delivery dates.
* @param {range} actualDates The range containing actual
delivery dates.
* @return {array | string} An array listing each order with its
delivery time deviation in days, or an error message if data is
invalid.
* @customfunction
*/
function CALCULATE_DELIVERY_DEVIATIONS(orderIDs,
expectedDates, actualDates) {
  const results = [];
for (let i = 0; i < orderIDs.length; i++) {
  const orderID = orderIDs[i][0];
  const expectedDate = new Date(expectedDates[i][0]);
  const actualDate = new Date(actualDates[i][0]);
  const deviation = (actualDate - expectedDate) / (1000 * 3600 *
24); // Convert milliseconds to days
  results.push([orderID, deviation]);
}
  return results.length > 0 ? results : "No delivery data
available.";
}
```

Steps:

1. Paste the code into a new Apps Script project.
2. Save the changes and return to Google Sheets.
3. Enter the sample data into columns A1:C6.
4. Use the function like
   =CALCULATE_DELIVERY_DEVIATIONS(A2:A6,
   B2:B6, C2:C6).

Expected Result: The function will return each order's delivery time deviation in days, indicating whether the delivery was early, late, or on time relative to the expected date.

Calculate Meeting Room Utilization

	A	B	C	D	E
1	Room	Total Hours Available	Hours Used		
2	Conference	50	30	Conference	60.00%
3	Boardroom	50	20	Boardroom	40.00%
4	Training	50	45	Training	90.00%
5	Executive	50	25	Executive	50.00%

Objective: Develop a function to calculate the percentage of time a meeting room is utilized based on its availability and the total duration of meetings held in it.

Sample Data:

Room	Total Hours Available	Hours Used
Conference	50	30
Boardroom	50	20
Training	50	45
Executive	50	25

Learning Outcomes:
- Learn to calculate utilization rates.
- Practice performing division and percentage calculations.

Code Example:
```
/**
 * Calculates the percentage of utilization for meeting rooms.
 *
 * @param {range} rooms The range containing room names.
 * @param {range} totalHoursAvailable The range containing
total hours available for each room.
```

* @param {range} hoursUsed The range containing the
number of hours each room was used.
* @return {array | string} An array listing each room with its
utilization percentage, or an error message if data is invalid.
* @customfunction
*/

```
function CALCULATE_ROOM_UTILIZATION(rooms,
totalHoursAvailable, hoursUsed) {
 const results = [];
 for (let i = 0; i < rooms.length; i++) {
 const room = rooms[i][0];
 const totalAvailable = totalHoursAvailable[i][0];
 const used = hoursUsed[i][0];
 const utilizationRate = (used / totalAvailable) * 100;
 results.push([room, utilizationRate.toFixed(2) + "%"]);
 }
 return results.length > 0 ? results : "Invalid or empty data!";
}
```

Steps:

1. Paste the code into a new Apps Script project.
2. Save the changes and return to Google Sheets.
3. Enter the sample data into columns A1:C5.
4. Use the function like
    =CALCULATE_ROOM_UTILIZATION(A2:A5, B2:B5,
    C2:C5).

Expected Result: The function will provide the utilization
percentage for each meeting room, highlighting how
effectively each space is being used.

Monitor Project Milestone Deadlines

	A	B	C	D	E	F
1	Project	Milestone	Due Date			
2	Project A	Design Phase	2024-05-10	Project D	Implementation	2024-05-29
3	Project B	Development	2024-05-05			
4	Project C	Testing	2024-05-15			
5	Project D	Implementation	2024-05-29			
6	Project E	Review	2024-05-02			

Objective: Write a function to list project milestones that are approaching within the next 7 days.

Sample Data:

Project	Milestone	Due Date
Project A	Design Phase	2024-05-10
Project B	Development	2024-05-05
Project C	Testing	2024-05-15
Project D	Implementation	2024-05-03
Project E	Review	2024-05-02

Learning Outcomes:
- Practice comparing dates to identify upcoming deadlines.
- Learn to manipulate and format date data for reporting.

Code Example:

```
/**
* Lists project milestones that are due within the next 7 days.
*
* @param {range} projects The range containing project names.
* @param {range} milestones The range containing milestone names.
* @param {range} dueDates The range containing due dates for each milestone.
* @return {array | string} An array listing projects with upcoming milestones, or an error message if no upcoming deadlines are found.
```

```
 * @customfunction
 */
function MONITOR_MILESTONE_DEADLINES(projects,
milestones, dueDates) {
 const today = new Date();
 const oneWeekLater = new Date(today.getFullYear(),
today.getMonth(), today.getDate() + 7);
 const results = [];
for (let i = 0; i < projects.length; i++) {
 const project = projects[i][0];
 const milestone = milestones[i][0];
 const dueDate = new Date(dueDates[i][0]);
 if (dueDate >= today && dueDate <= oneWeekLater) {
 results.push([project, milestone,
dueDate.toISOString().split('T')[0]]);
 }
 }
 return results.length > 0 ? results : "No upcoming milestones
within the next 7 days.";
 }
```

Steps:

1. Paste the code into a new Apps Script project.
2. Save the changes and return to Google Sheets.
3. Enter the sample data into columns A1:C6.
4. Adjust the system date for testing, if necessary, and use the function like =MONITOR_MILESTONE_DEADLINES(A2:A6, B2:B6, C2:C6).

Expected Result: The function will list projects that have milestones approaching within the next week.

Analyze Customer Feedback Trends

C2 ▾ fx =ANALYZE_FEEDBACK_TRENDS(A2:A6, B2:B6)

	A	B	C	D	E
1	Month	Feedback Score			
2	January	78	February	Improving	4
3	February	82	March	Declining	-2
4	March	80	April	Improving	5
5	April	85	May	Improving	3
6	May	88			

Objective: Create a function to analyze the trend in customer feedback scores over multiple months.

Sample Data:

Month	Feedback Score
January	78
February	82
March	80
April	85
May	88

Learning Outcomes:
- Learn to analyze trends in sequential data.
- Practice numerical comparisons and trend analysis.

Code Example:

```
/**
 * Analyzes trends in customer feedback scores over months.
 *
 * @param {range} months The range containing month
names.
 * @param {range} scores The range containing feedback
scores.
 * @return {array | string} An array listing each month with
the change in score from the previous month, or an error
message if data is invalid.
 * @customfunction
```

```
*/
function ANALYZE_FEEDBACK_TRENDS(months, scores) {
  const results = [];
for (let i = 1; i < scores.length; i++) {
  const previousScore = scores[i - 1][0];
  const currentScore = scores[i][0];
  const change = currentScore - previousScore;
  const trend = change > 0 ? "Improving" : change < 0 ?
"Declining" : "Stable";
  results.push([months[i][0], trend, change]);
  }
  return results.length > 0 ? results : "Insufficient data for trend
analysis.";
}
```

Steps:

1. Paste the code into a new Apps Script project.
2. Save the changes and return to Google Sheets.
3. Enter the sample data into columns A1:B6.
4. Use the function like
    =ANALYZE_FEEDBACK_TRENDS(A2:A6, B2:B6).

Expected Result: The function will analyze month-over-month changes in customer feedback scores, providing insights into whether customer satisfaction is improving, declining, or remaining stable.

Calculate Average Daily Revenue

C2	▾	fx =CALCULATE_AVERAGE_DAILY_REVENUE(A2:A6, B2:B6)

	A	B	C	D
1	Store	Revenue (Monthly)		
2	Store A	30000	Store A	$1000.00
3	Store B	45000	Store B	$1500.00
4	Store C	25000	Store C	$833.33
5	Store D	32000	Store D	$1066.67
6	Store E	43000	Store E	$1433.33

Objective: Develop a function to calculate the average daily revenue for each store over a month.

Sample Data:

Store	Revenue (Monthly)
Store A	30000
Store B	45000
Store C	25000
Store D	32000
Store E	43000

Learning Outcomes:
- Learn to calculate average values based on monthly data.
- Practice dividing total sums by the number of units (days in this case).

Code Example:

```
/**
 * Calculates average daily revenue for each store.
 *
 * @param {range} stores The range containing store names.
 * @param {range} monthlyRevenue The range containing
 monthly revenue figures.
 * @return {array|string} An array listing each store with its
 average daily revenue, assuming a 30-day month, or an error
 message if data is invalid.
 * @customfunction
 */
function
CALCULATE_AVERAGE_DAILY_REVENUE(stores,
monthlyRevenue) {
 const daysInMonth = 30; // Assuming 30 days in the month
for simplicity
 const results = [];
 for (let i = 0; i < stores.length; i++) {
 const store = stores[i][0];
```

```
const revenue = monthlyRevenue[i][0];
const averageDailyRevenue = (revenue /
daysInMonth).toFixed(2);
results.push([store, `$${averageDailyRevenue}`]);
}
return results.length > 0 ? results : "Invalid or empty data!";
}
```

Steps:

1. Paste the code into a new Apps Script project.
2. Save the changes and return to Google Sheets.
3. Enter the sample data into columns A1:B6.
4. Use the function like
   =CALCULATE_AVERAGE_DAILY_REVENUE(A2:A
   6, B2:B6).

Expected Result: The function will provide the average daily revenue for each store, helping to understand daily sales performance.

Acknowledgments

The creation of "Google Sheets Custom Functions with Apps Script,: Over 150 Apps Script Code Examples for Sheets" represents a collective endeavor driven by passion and unwavering commitment. This work is made possible through the valuable contributions and relentless support of many remarkable individuals whose expertise and encouragement have been essential.

First and foremost, my deepest thanks go to the dynamic Google Apps Script community. Your insights, shared experiences, and unwavering collaborative spirit have been crucial in shaping this book. This volume is a homage to our community's collective wisdom and fellowship.

I owe immense gratitude to my family and friends for their constant support and understanding throughout this project. Your faith in my vision has been a beacon of guidance and encouragement.

To you, the reader, I offer my heartfelt thanks for joining this journey of discovery and mastery. This book is crafted to facilitate your growth and success as a Google Apps Script developer, celebrating your dedication to refining your skills, which in turn enriches our shared craft.

Together, we forge ahead, expanding the horizons of what we can achieve with Google Apps Script. I am grateful for your pivotal role in this ongoing adventure.

With profound appreciation,

Laurence Lars Svekis

About the Author

Laurence Lars Svekis is an accomplished web developer, esteemed online educator, and innovative entrepreneur, celebrated for his significant contributions to technology and digital education. With a rich background spanning over twenty years in web application development, Laurence stands as a pivotal figure in the realm of online learning, equipping a global audience with his extensive knowledge.

As a recognized Google Developer Expert for Workspace and a passionate proponent of Google Apps Script, Laurence combines deep technical expertise with a fervent zeal for teaching. He is best known for his top-rated courses on Google Apps Script, through which he imparts actionable insights and practical knowledge drawn from his robust experience in both development and education. Moreover, Laurence actively engages with the Apps Script community, enhancing collaboration and the exchange of knowledge among developers.

His dedication to education is evident in his milestone of educating over one million students worldwide, a clear indicator of the impact and efficacy of his instructional approach. Laurence's courses span a wide range of web development topics, designed to support learners of all levels in their programming endeavors.

In addition to his educational pursuits, Laurence is a prolific author whose publications resonate with his educational ethos of simplicity and approachability. His books offer readers practical strategies to master the intricacies of web development and programming, ensuring an engaging and fruitful learning experience.

Motivated by a love for technology and a drive for innovation, Laurence continues to venture into new areas of web technology, creating solutions that tackle real-world problems. His commitment to disseminating knowledge and empowering others highlights his leadership and visionary status in the digital world.

In essence, Laurence Lars Svekis is a pioneering web developer, influential educator, best-selling author, and forward-thinking entrepreneur. His enduring contributions have profoundly influenced the field of web development, inspiring a multitude of learners to achieve their fullest potential in the ever-evolving digital arena.

For more content and to learn more, visit
https://basescripts.com/

Book Source Code on GitHub
https://github.com/lsvekis/Sheets-Custom-Formulas-Book